W9-BKO-578

# Fear

## R. T. KENDALL

CHARISMA HOUSE

Most Charisma Media products are available at special quantity discounts for bulk purchase for sales promotions, premiums, fund-raising, and educational needs. For details, call us at (407) 333-0600 or visit our website at www.charismamedia.com.

FEAR by R. T. Kendall
Published by Charisma House, an imprint of Charisma Media
600 Rinehart Road, Lake Mary, Florida 32746

*In memory of Dr. Gene E. Phillips (1902–1977)*

# Contents

# Foreword

IN 2005 I was browsing through a Christian Book Distributors catalog and spotted a book with an intriguing title, *In Pursuit of His Glory*, written by R. T. Kendall, a man I had never heard of. It ignited a curiosity in me, for that's exactly what my heart's desire is, to bring God glory by the life I live. I read the book and was impacted by RT's stories of being the pastor at prestigious Westminster Chapel in London. His raw honesty and integrity encouraged and inspired me. The things he learned and the things he would do again touched a nerve in my heart.

I decided that RT was someone I wanted to come and preach at Island Church, so I contacted him and invited him to come. His first visit, in 2005, was amazing when he preached on total forgiveness! So began a friendship with RT and his wife, Louise, that my wife, Jenni, and I treasure to this day. We have been blessed to welcome RT and Louise to Island Church every year since that memorable Sunday, July 17, 2005. Consequently, I have read all RT's books and always look forward to the insights and revelation he shares from the depth of his experience living the Christian life and his love for God and His people.

The fear of God has gone missing from the Western church. Churches that focus on programs rather than His presence don't know what you are talking about when you mention the fear of God. They assume you are talking about behavior modification rather than a heart response to the greatness of God. With churches lost in the blur of doing ministry instead of enjoying being in His presence, the awe and wonder of God have been relegated to a bygone era, the fear of God reduced to a God they don't know.

This book, *Fear*, is classic R. T. Kendall writing with thought-provoking accuracy, just as a surgeon precisely uses his tools of trade. RT is seeking to awaken the church to the wonder and awe of our majestic and holy God to help prepare us for the day we stand before Him. Using personal examples of his own failures and short-comings and successes, this book is an invitation to go deeper in your walk with God—a God who longs for our relationship, who has spread a table for us to feast from, who has prepared more for us than all we could ask, think, or even imagine. Having a healthy fear of God will grow us up into a maturity that will open up the door to experience His glory and a revelation of His magnificent goodness.

Many of the books I have by RT are signed with John 5:44 as the encouraging scripture. RT has sought to live a life to bring God honor and glory. He seeks God's opinion (glory, *doxa*) over his life. God has appointed a day for every single human being where we will stand before Him and give accounts of our lives and He will give His opinion of the lives we have lived. We all hope and pray that we will hear this opinion of God: "Well done, good and faithful servant. Enter into the joy of your Master."

The fear of man (bad fear) is a huge trap that many get ensnared by. In fact, it paralyzes people and renders them powerless, where they bow to the pressures of what others think. I have been such a victim, and I can assure you, it's not a good place to live. Like RT, I used to go fishing for compliments, hoping someone would say something encouraging to me.

In our COVID-19 world, the fear of what others think has been escalated to new heights, capturing many in its snare. The fear of man manifests in so many different ways, causing its victims to succumb to lies that numb their hearts to the reality of God's very great and precious promises. RT skillfully helps those trapped to escape and live on God's promises by focusing on eternal realities.

We are at war! In March 2020 everything got ramped up. Jesus is coming again soon, and the devil is filled with such fury that he unleashed on the human race a level of spiritual warfare unseen before. His goal is to cause many to lose hope, faith, and love, and his mission is to steal, kill, and destroy.

Many have sadly bowed to his attacks, bowed to his fear, and walked away from the faith. Isolation is his objective, and that's where the damage is done. Alone we lose hope. Alone our faith shrinks. Alone our love for God and others dries up. We need to gather together as the church without fear, to praise God and to love others. The devil fears the gathered church and is doing all he can to stop us being together.

Living in the fear of God now prepares me for the day when I will stand before our glorious Savior. May this book inspire you afresh to live for God's glory, just as it has me.

—PASTOR GRANT BREWSTER
ISLAND CHURCH
BAINBRIDGE ISLAND, WASHINGTON

# Preface

THE FILM *THE Good, the Bad and the Ugly* became a very popular movie. The star, Clint Eastwood, plays the role of one who was not in fact a very good man, but good only by comparing him to the bad man—played by Lee Van Cleef—and the ugly man, played by Eli Wallach. Although comparisons are onerous, I ask for your indulgence for my borrowing the famous movie title in order to demonstrate three kinds of fear: the fear of God (the good), the fear of man (the bad), and satanic fear (the ugly).

I want to say first of all that I have prayed for you. I have prayed that everyone who reads this book will have the protection that comes from the sprinkling of the blood of Christ (1 Pet. 1:2; Heb. 12:24). I would like to think that the devil is unhappy with all of my books, but I can assure you that he will not like this one—especially the third section.

I thank Charisma Media for the privilege of writing another book with them. Steve and Joy Strang, owners of Charisma Media, have been special friends for over twenty-five years and have published more than twenty of my books. My warm thanks to Debbie Marrie, my editor, who has been an encourager and helpful critic over the years—and has been terrific in helping me with this one.

I have prayed that God would enable me to write this book as if it were my only one—and last one. I admit my tendency is to think that my current book is the most important. But please understand that the subject of this book is most grave and very timely. I pray that you will be gripped as I have been.

I dedicate this book to the memory of Dr. Gene E. Phillips, my first pastor. As you will read below, his influence on me when I was a child was profound. It happens that his son, Dr. Gene C. Phillips, was my first friend and certainly therefore oldest as well. Following in his father's footsteps, he became a Nazarene pastor as well. We are both eighty-six. I had the privilege of reading the opening words of this book on the telephone to "Genie," as I called him. I trust this book will bless Genie and all of you who read what follows.

I thank Debbie Marrie for her encouragement and wisdom in her usual acute suggestions and for Steve Strang in allowing me to do another book with Charisma Media. Most of all, I thank Louise—my best friend and critic—for her encouragement.

—R. T. KENDALL
NASHVILLE
AUGUST 2021

# Introduction

I HAD A HEAD start when it comes to the fear of the Lord. Between my parental background and my church background, I was given a double dose of the sense of the fear of God.

I am reminded too of the famous quote of William Booth (1829–1912), founder of The Salvation Army:

> I consider that the chief dangers which confront the coming century will be religion without the Holy Ghost, Christianity without Christ, forgiveness without repentance, salvation without regeneration, politics without God, and heaven without hell.

In the introduction to his book *God's Hell*, William Booth referred to his address to the first graduating class of The Salvation Army officers. He stated that perhaps he should apologize for keeping them for two years in order to teach them how to win a soul to Jesus Christ. It would have been better, he said, had they "spent five minutes in hell."

My church in Ashland, Kentucky (Church of the Nazarene), was born in the kind of preaching that would have blessed William Booth. I cut my teeth on this kind of theology including the preaching on hell. Jesus had

1

more to say about hell than He did about heaven, and so too my old church. I have often wondered if the atmosphere of my old church in Ashland was the last vestige of the historic Cane Ridge Revival (which I will mention below), some one hundred miles away.

I vividly remember an event when I was seven or eight years old. We were coming out of church after our Wednesday night prayer meeting at First Church of the Nazarene in Ashland. Our pastor was the Rev. Gene Phillips. As far back as I can remember, every time I heard him preach a sense of the fear of God came over me. That Wednesday night as we were heading home I noticed that the full moon was red. My father then said, "When the moon is the color of blood it is a sign of the second coming." He was referring to biblical verses such as "the moon became as blood" (Acts 2:20; Rev. 6:12). I feared that the second coming would come any minute, and I was afraid I wasn't ready.

I was terrified. I could not go to sleep that night until I confessed all my sins to God. I don't remember what these sins were, but they were real to me then. When I confessed them, I had peace—and went off to sleep. The truth is, the moon on that Wednesday night had the color of blood because of the nearby Armco steel mill; the smoke of the furnaces changed the moon's color to red for some reason. Even though there was nothing supernatural about the moon's color, I am thankful that I had a tender conscience. Although I now have a full assurance of my salvation, I pray that I will never lose the fear of displeasing the Lord. Paul admonished us to "try to discern what is pleasing to the Lord" (Eph. 5:10). Enoch had this witness before his translation to heaven that he "pleased God" (Heb. 11:5). I am *so* thankful that I have not (so far) outgrown that desire.

I still think a lot about my Nazarene background. Dr. Martyn Lloyd-Jones, one of my predecessors at Westminster Chapel, used to urge me, "Don't forget your Nazarene background—it is what has saved you." He had read the biography of Phineas Bresee (1838–1915), the founder of the Church of the Nazarene, and sensed a genuineness among Nazarenes. By saying, "This is what has saved you," he was not referring to how I was saved but comparing me to so many reformed ministers who, he would say, were "perfectly orthodox, perfectly useless." Here is one of the huge differences between old Nazarenes and some of the churches I have encountered: I grew up with a burning desire to please the Lord. I am not their judge, of course, but I fear that this desire to please God is absent in so many places today.

When I was fifteen, we had a guest evangelist at our church—Dr. W. M. Tidwell. He was a bit eccentric but also a legend in the Nazarene movement. (When I went to Trevecca Nazarene College a few years later, my dormitory was called Tidwell Hall, named after him.) On the final Sunday morning of the two-week meeting in Ashland, I was called out of the Sunday school class that preceded the main service. Dr. Tidwell wanted to see me. He said he planned to preach on the parable about the man who did not have the wedding garment and was then bound "hand and foot" and cast into outer darkness where there would be weeping and gnashing of teeth (Matt. 22:13). He wanted to use me as a visible illustration. At a certain moment in his sermon, he would motion for me to take a seat in front of the congregation. Then four men in the congregation that day, to illustrate the rest of the parable, had been designated to tie my hands and feet and then carry me up the center aisle and out of the church—as an example of the man in the parable who did not have the wedding garment and was sent to outer darkness.

People afterward spoke of the solemnity that came over the service. Except for possibly one person, a teenaged girl—Patsy Branham. My mother, who sat near her, particularly remembered that Patsy was irreverent and disrespectful—even mocking during the preaching—and laughed at me as the four men were carrying me out of the church. While an invitational hymn was being sung, old Dr. Tidwell asked that the singing stop. "Someone here is getting their final call," he said as the congregation stood. He refused to close the service but turned things over to the pastor, who also would not dismiss the service. People sat down and slowly got up and went to their homes.

The next day, as I came home from delivering the newspaper *Ashland Daily Independent*, which I did every day, my mother was waiting on the front porch for me.

"Did you hear about Patsy?" she asked with anxiety and tears.

"No, what do you mean?" I asked.

"Patsy was killed an hour ago as she was walking home from school." A speeding car rammed into another car, which careened onto the sidewalk and hit Patsy, who was killed instantly.

I knew Patsy. I was stunned. She was only sixteen. Would God hold a sweet little teenaged girl responsible for her attitude and actions? Haven't we all been guilty of the same sort of mockery at one time or another? Why would the Holy Spirit lead Dr. Tidwell to say, "Someone is getting their last call" (by which he meant last opportunity to respond positively to God's invitation to be saved)? Was Patsy being singled out? Was God really telling all of us that someone present was going to be lost if they did not respond? I have asked questions like these many times since.

The answer is yes. Rather than quarrel with God, I bow to this truth:

> "For my thoughts are not your thoughts, neither are your ways my ways," declares the LORD. "For as the heavens are higher than the earth, so are my ways higher than your ways and my thoughts than your thoughts."
>
> —ISAIAH 55:8–9

I would add: one's last or final call implies that one had been warned previously.

A good number of people spontaneously went to the

church that Monday evening, just to be with each other. All were sobered and quiet. Everyone was thinking the same thing, recalling old Dr. Tidwell's warning, "Someone here is getting their final call."

That occasion had an effect on me to this day that I have never completely got over. Strange as this may seem, between the impact of that Sunday service led by Dr. Tidwell plus the preaching and influence of Gene Phillips, I have never lost a sense of the fear of the Lord. Whenever I return to Ashland, I make it a point to drive by 25th and Montgomery Avenue to have a look at the corner and spot where Patsy was killed.

As for Patsy Branham's being taken suddenly after being warned in that church service, which seems strange and unfair to some, I have much the same sort of question regarding the sins of King Saul and King David. King Saul was punished for merely abusing the ceremonial law regarding burnt offerings, which he was not supposed to offer. God rejected him from that moment (1 Sam. 13:8–14). His life after that was horrible and ended in tragedy (1 Sam. 31:4–6). King David committed adultery with Bathsheba. She became pregnant. David then killed her husband, Uriah, to cover up his sin (2 Sam. 11). That to me seems a thousand times worse than Saul's sin. But David was forgiven and restored and forever regarded as Israel's greatest king.

I made a decision a long time ago not to question God's ways. I certainly don't understand many of them. But I bow to Him. I have never been sorry for this.

On the other hand, I have watched people who chose to question God's ways with anger and bitterness and denied the truth of the Bible. And then I have seen their end, nearly always ending in sadness. I have observed those who came to seminary believing the Bible but embraced existentialism. None of them that I know of succeeded in the ministry, and many left the ministry.

## I HAVE CHOSEN THE FEAR OF THE LORD

The church today is generally losing its young people by the hundreds of thousands. The age they begin to desert the faith is around sixteen. Very few young people brought up in church these days remain there. Why? No fear of God. Were they to see how angry God is with their mocking and frivolity, it would result in a change of attitude.

I would also observe that the young people in my old church in Ashland who were of the same age and generation as Patsy *stayed in the church*. And continued to walk with the Lord. Most are now in heaven. I am the only one (that I know of) still alive. I can recall no one—young or old—who deserted the church owing to Dr. Tidwell's warning or Patsy's sudden death. It had the opposite effect. Furthermore, Patsy's sister followed the Lord and later married a man who became a Nazarene minister. Patsy's own father became a Christian after Patsy died.

While in high school in Ashland, part of our reading

included a section of Jonathan Edwards' (1703–1758) sermon "Sinners in the Hands of an Angry God." Some of the students snickered as they read certain lines, such as, "It is by the mercy of God that you are not in hell now." But no one was laughing in the congregational church in Enfield, Connecticut, on July 8, 1741. Taking his text from Deuteronomy 32:35, "Their foot shall slide in due time" (KJV), Edwards read his sermon from a manuscript. He had no oratory or charisma. But the people began to moan and groan. Edwards tried to get the people to be quiet, but by the time he finished many were holding on to the church pews to keep from *sliding* into hell. So great was the power of the Spirit that strong men were seen holding on to tree trunks outside the church to keep from sliding into hell.

News of the sermon and its effect went all over New England in days. It went all over England in weeks. Edwards tried preaching it again in his own church in Northampton, Massachusetts. No effect whatever followed. *God only did it once.* Once was enough to shake New England. It is what many think of when they think of the Great Awakening (1735–1750). Solid research has shown that the Great Awakening led to the Declaration of Independence (1776).

One can only wonder what it will be like when we stand before God at the judgment seat of Christ to give an account of our lives, including the deeds done in the body (2 Cor. 5:10). In fact, a Methodist lay preacher stood on a fallen tree on a Sunday morning—August 8,

1801—and took 2 Corinthians 5:10 as his text before fifteen thousand people. A sense of the fear of God was so strong that hundreds fell spontaneously to the ground. Nobody had prayed that people would fall, or "swoon" as it was referred to then. No one pushed them. Between that Sunday and Wednesday there were never fewer than five hundred people prostrate on the ground. But they would come out of it in hours shouting with assurance of salvation. Their voices could be heard a mile away. It was called "the sound of Niagara," this—known as the Cane Ridge Revival—being America's second Great Awakening. Both awakenings were characterized by an eschatological emphasis.

Louise and I have visited the spot in Enfield four times. We drove two hours out of our way just to stand or kneel on the vacant lot where the original church was located in Enfield, across from the Montessori school there, praying, "O Lord, do it again."

I wish I could testify that I have seen the evidence of the fear of God displayed throughout my ministry. I haven't. For this reason, in some ways I feel like a fraud in writing this book. I would gladly step aside and welcome someone to write on this subject who has far more experience of this phenomenon than I have.

I do not think it is an exaggeration to say that the greatest need of the church today is a return of the fear of the Lord. I do not think it is an exaggeration to say that the greatest absence in the church today is the fear of God.

The nearest I have come in my adult life to seeing the fear of God before my eyes was on two separate occasions at Westminster Chapel. Preaching on the life of David, I came to the story of Nabal and Abigail. Nabal, a wealthy man, refused to show mercy to David, who needed food for his men. David decided to get revenge, but Abigail, Nabal's wife, interceded and pleaded successfully with David not to go after Nabal. She waited for Nabal, who had been "merry" while holding a feast, to get sober. Then she told him what David had planned to do and how she stopped him. Nabal's heart "failed him and he became like a stone." And about ten days later "the LORD struck Nabal and he died" (1 Sam. 25:37–38, NIV, the translation I used then).

As soon as the service was over, an unmarried couple in their twenties came immediately to see me in the vestry. They were clearly shaken. The man was trembling in fear. They both prayed to receive the Lord then and there. A few weeks later they revealed that they had stopped living together. They asked me to marry them. I did. Later they were baptized and became staunch members of Westminster Chapel.

The second occasion was when a lady who had been reading my book *God Meant It for Good* came to hear me preach. At the beginning of the first service, she came to me, and I for some reason quoted 1 Corinthians 10:13: "No temptation has overtaken you except what is common to mankind. And God is faithful and he will not let you be tempted beyond what you can bear. But when you are tempted, he will also provide a way out so that you can endure it" (NIV). The lady was converted the same evening. She said the fear of God came on her as I read that verse. She was convinced that I could see right through her. I did not see her at all! It was an effectual work of grace; that woman became one of the most godly I have seen throughout my ministry.

I do not believe that all those converted under my preaching were necessarily motivated by the fear of God. The preaching of the wrath of God is not the only way people are led to Christ. Peter talked about a wife winning her husband by her "conduct" (1 Pet. 3:1–2). Paul said much the same thing when he urged husbands and wives to stay together even if one is not saved. "For how do you know, wife, whether you will save your husband? Or how do you know, husband, whether you will save your wife?" (1 Cor. 7:16). These things said, the principal reason Paul gave for the gospel being the power of God for salvation is the wrath of God (Rom. 1:16, 18). Millions can sing the first verse of "Amazing Grace" from memory, but few can remember the words of the second verse:

> 'Twas grace that taught my heart to fear,
> and grace my fears relieved;
> how precious did that grace appear
> the hour I first believed!
>
> —JOHN NEWTON (1725–1807)[1]

# PART I

# The Good—
# the Fear of God

## CHAPTER 1

# The Eternal Gospel

Then I saw another angel flying in midair, and he
had the eternal gospel to proclaim to those who
live on the earth—to every nation, tribe, language
and people. He said in a loud voice, "Fear God
and give him glory, because the hour of his judgment has come. Worship him who made the heavens,
the earth, the sea and the springs of water."

—REVELATION 14:6–7 (NIV)

The superstars in heaven will be people
we never heard of on earth.

—GRAHAM KENDRICK

MY FATHER TOLD me the following story many
times. He and my mother, who was six months
pregnant with me, were in a Nazarene church in Indianapolis. My dad was so gripped by the sermon that he
put his hand on my mother's tummy and prayed, "Lord,
let my son preach like this man" (he was counting on my
being a son!).

Almost twenty years later a visiting chapel preacher

at Trevecca Nazarene College (now university) preached a sermon based on Hebrews 11:5 (KJV): "By faith Enoch was translated that he should not see death; and was not found, because God had translated him: for before his translation he had this testimony, that he pleased God." It is the only chapel sermon during my entire time at Trevecca that I remember. I can still remember the main points. The focus in a nutshell: *Enoch pleased God, but not necessarily people.* I was so shaken and stirred by that sermon that I went immediately to my dormitory room, knelt at my bed, and prayed that somehow I might truly please God. I then phoned my dad to tell him about the sermon.

"Who was the preacher?" my father asked.

"A preacher called C. B. Cox."

My father then replied, "C. B. Cox was the preacher I was listening to when I prayed for you in Indianapolis."

The fear of God does not mean that God is afraid. Whereas the love of God refers to His love, the justice of God to His justice, and the wrath of God to His anger, the fear of God refers to *our fear of Him.* Does this mean we should be afraid of God? Partly, yes. We preachers nowadays are, first, not very prone to talk about the fear of God and, second, if we do, we want to say to the people: "But this does not mean we should be afraid of Him." Really? I think we should when fearing God is properly understood. When we get to heaven and watch a video recording of the preaching of John the Baptist, it would not surprise me to learn that many of his hearers were nearly scared to death from his preaching.

## THAT IS WHAT THIS BOOK IS LARGELY ABOUT

It seems to me that the preaching of the fear of God and Jesus' own teaching of eternal punishment have been largely avoided because we are afraid people won't come back to church. The truth is, the fear of displeasing people by camouflaging the fear of God is what is partly responsible for emptying churches.

It is easy to forget that the first sermon in the New Testament was by John the Baptist: "Who warned you to *flee from the wrath to come?*" (Matt. 3:7, emphasis added). People walked or came on camels' backs for twenty miles to be told about the fear of God.

My schoolteacher back in Ashland, Kentucky, when having to comment on Jonathan Edwards' aforementioned sermon (it was in the literature books of those days), denounced Edwards' sermon and said that we should concentrate on the *love* of God. Because John 3:16, the Bible in a nutshell, says that God "so loved the world" that He gave His only son, that whoever would believe in Him should not perish but have eternal life, people understandably head straight for the reference to the love of God. But they forget that those who don't believe will "perish"—a reference to God's wrath and justice. God loved us so much that He sent His Son so we would not go to hell.

## GOD'S WAYS

A fair question is: If God does not want us to perish, why did He not simply destroy hell? He is the One who created it. Why did He not do away with hell? Could He not do that? Do you know the answer to that? I don't. Allow me to quote again these words:

> For my thoughts are not your thoughts, neither are your ways my ways, declares the LORD. For as the heavens are higher than the earth, so are my ways higher than your ways and my thoughts than your thoughts.
>
> —ISAIAH 55:8–9

We are at an intersection right here. You have come to the end of the road and must turn to the right or left. This is not like Yogi Berra's famous advice, "When you come to a fork in the road, take it."[1] You have a clear decision to make: to choose God's ways or stick with your ways. Simple as that.

God has "ways." He lamented that ancient Israel did not know His "ways" (Heb. 3:10). Moses' most earnest request was to know God's "ways" (Exod. 33:13). The prophet Isaiah exhorted:

> Come, let us go up to the mountain of the LORD, to the house of the God of Jacob, that he may teach us his ways and that we may walk in his paths.
>
> —ISAIAH 2:3

I must repeat: God has *ways*. These ways must be taught. "Come, O children, listen to me; I will teach you the fear of the LORD" (Ps. 34:11). God's ways, part of which is the fear of the Lord, must be taught. Why? Because *by nature* we have no sense of the fear of God. It is alien to us. This is why we naturally despise the notion of the fear of God.

> None is righteous, no, not one; no one under-stands; no one seeks for God....there is no fear of God before their eyes.
>
> —ROMANS 3:10–11, 18

## JOHANNINE LITERATURE

Almost certainly the least understood book in the Bible is Revelation. But some verses are plain and clear—like Revelation 14:7. The first two words contained in what is called the "eternal gospel" are "fear God."

Does this surprise you? It surprises me, to be honest. And yet all of Johannine literature (the Gospel of John, the letters of John, and the Book of Revelation) have this thread in common: the justice and anger of God; not only the need for someone to be saved but also to be obedient owing to the justice and wrath of God. What follows are some examples of this teaching.

> And making a whip of cords, he [Jesus] drove them all [those selling oxen, sheep and pigeons and the money-changers] out of the temple....He poured out the coins of the money-changers and overturned their tables. And he told those who

sold the pigeons, "Take these things away; do not make my Father's house a house of trade."

—JOHN 2:15–16

Jesus on his part did not entrust himself to them, because he knew all people and needed no one to bear witness about man, for he himself knew what was in man.

—JOHN 2:24–25

Truly, truly, I say to you, unless one is born again he cannot see the kingdom of God.

—JOHN 3:3

Do not marvel at this, for an hour is coming when all who are in the tombs will hear his voice and come out, those who have done good to the resurrection of life, and those who have done evil to the resurrection of judgment.

—JOHN 5:28–29

As Moses lifted up the serpent in the wilderness [so people would not perish from poisonous snakes, which God had sent because of His anger], so must the Son of Man be lifted up, that whoever believes in him may have eternal life.

—JOHN 3:14–15

For God so loved the world, that he gave his only Son, that whoever believes in him should not perish [that is, go to hell], but have eternal life.

—JOHN 3:16

Whoever does not believe [in the Son] is condemned already....This is the judgment: the light has come into the world, and people loved the darkness rather than the light because their works were evil.

—JOHN 3:18–19

Whoever believes in the Son has eternal life; whoever does not obey the Son shall not see life, but the wrath of God remains on him.

—JOHN 3:36

For this is the will of my Father, that everyone who looks on the Son and believes in him should have eternal life, and I will raise him up on the last day.

—JOHN 6:40

Unless you eat the flesh of the Son of Man and drink his blood, you have no life in you.

—JOHN 6:53

The one who rejects me and does not receive my words has a judge: the word that I have spoken will judge him on the last day.

—JOHN 12:48

When he [the Holy Spirit] comes, he will convict the world concerning sin and righteousness and judgment.

—JOHN 16:8

If we will confess our sins, he is faithful and just to forgive us our sins and cleanse us from all unrighteousness.

—1 JOHN 1:9

He is the propitiation for our sins.

—1 JOHN 2:2

He loved us and sent his Son to be the propitiation for our sins.

—1 JOHN 4:10

We may have confidence for the day of judgment.

—1 JOHN 4:17

There is a sin that leads to death.

—1 JOHN 5:16

I will remove your lampstand from its place, unless you repent.

—REVELATION 2:5

Therefore repent. If not, I will come to you soon and war against them with the sword of my mouth.

—REVELATION 2:16

Behold, I will throw her onto a sickbed, and those who commit adultery with her I will throw into great tribulation, unless they repent of her works.

—REVELATION 2:22

If you will not wake up, I will come like a thief, and you will not know at what hour I will come against you.

—REVELATION 3:3

I will make those of the synagogue of Satan who say that they are Jews and are not, but lie— behold, I will make them come and bow down before your feet.

—REVELATION 3:9

So, because you are lukewarm, and neither hot nor cold, I will spit you out of my mouth.

—REVELATION 3:16

Those whom I love, I reprove and discipline.

—REVELATION 3:19

Then the kings of the earth and the great ones and the generals and the rich and the powerful, and everyone, slave and free, hid themselves in the caves and among the rocks of the mountains, calling to the mountains and rocks, "Fall on us and hide us from the face of him who is seated on the throne, and from the wrath of the Lamb, for the great day of their wrath has come, and who can stand?"

—REVELATION 6:15–17

He will be tormented with fire and sulfur in the presence of the holy angels and in the presence of the Lamb. And the smoke of their torment goes up forever and ever, and they have no rest, day or night.

—REVELATION 14:10–11

And I saw the dead, great and small, standing before the throne, and the books were opened. Then another book was opened which is the

> book of life. And the dead were judged by what
> was written in the books, according to what they
> had done....And if anyone's name was not found
> written in the book of life, he was thrown into the
> lake of fire.
>
> —REVELATION 20:12, 15

I do not claim to understand all these verses. But the link that holds them together is the justice of God. Like it or not, God is just. It should be noted that God is faithful and *just* to forgive our sins. Why "just"? Because God is a God who demands justice and needs to be propitiated. The word "propitiation" in 1 John 2:2 and 1 John 4:10 means that the blood of Jesus has turned God's wrath away from our sins. In other words, God's justice was *satisfied* by the life and death of His Son Jesus Christ. That is why God can forgive our sins and be true to Himself.

## THE GOSPEL

The word *gospel* is used seventy-seven times in the New Testament but only once in Johannine literature. And it is there called the "eternal gospel" and with an angel crying with a "loud voice," saying:

> Fear God and give him glory, because the hour
> of his judgment has come, and worship him who
> made heaven and earth, the sea and the springs
> of water.
>
> —REVELATION 14:7

The Book of Revelation is "the revelation of Jesus Christ" (Rev. 1:1). Not revelations, plural, but revelation. The book reveals the *true Jesus*—past, present, future; His person and His work. The word *eternal,* or *everlasting,* means that it is never-changing and there is only one gospel. It would likewise be the "same" Jesus as in the four Gospels. It is noteworthy that the first thing the angel crying with a loud voice says is "Fear God."

Think about that: "fear God." The eternal gospel is a command to fear God.

Does this surprise you? And yet, as I said, it does me! But it shouldn't. When the gospel of the kingdom is first unveiled in the New Testament, Jesus' words are "Repent, for the kingdom of heaven is at hand" (Matt. 4:17). The word *repent* in the New Testament implies one should change their ways because of the nature of God. He is a holy, jealous God. Changing our ways comes to this: fear God.

Indeed, the first message of John the Baptist was "flee from the wrath to come" (Matt. 3:7). The first word of Jesus' preaching was "Repent" (Matt. 4:17).

Never forget that Jesus never—ever—apologized for the God of the Old Testament. The God of the Old Testament was His Father. The God of the Old Testament is a jealous God. God unashamedly said that His name is "Jealous" (Exod. 34:14).

The only reference to the gospel in the Book of Revelation (Rev. 14:6–7) is to *fear God.*

## THE GLORY OF GOD

There is more: give glory to Him. The word *glory* comes from the Greek *doxa*, meaning "praise" or "honor." John's use of *doxa* is best understood by Jesus' words in John 5:44: "How can you believe, when you receive glory from one another and do not seek the glory that comes from the only God?" If you have read many of my books, you will know that I have sought to let this be my governing verse in life, beginning over sixty years ago.

The glory of God and the jealousy of God may often be used interchangeably. God is jealous and will not allow us to worship any other god but only Him. This is one of His ways; that is the way He is. Furthermore, He wants *all* the praise, honor, and glory for saving us. The same God who said to Moses, "I will have mercy on whom I will have mercy" (Exod. 33:19; Rom. 9:15) is the same God who has saved us. He did not have to save us. He could have passed us by and been equally just. The hymn writer Fanny Crosby (1820–1915) knew this very well. This is why she penned the hymn:

> Pass me not, O gentle Savior, hear my humble cry;
> While on others Thou art calling, do not pass
> me by.[2]

The carnal mind does not like this aspect of God's ways. When I was studying in a theological seminary many years ago, I was surprised to hear of so many students objecting to a God who wanted praise and glory.

This is why Jonathan Edwards said that the one thing the devil cannot produce in us is a love for the glory of God. That means if you love the glory and honor of God, be encouraged to know that *only God* could have put it there! This means that you are truly saved.

And yet, as Detective Columbo might say, "Oh, there is one more thing": the eternal gospel is a command not only to fear God and give Him glory, but also to "worship him who made heaven and earth, the sea and the springs of water" (Rev. 14:7). God wants our worship. He wants our praise. He wants us to keep our eyes on Him, to set our affection on things above, not on things of the earth (Col. 3:1). It means a lifelong commitment to praise Him, thank Him, and put Him first in our lives. As we have been noticing, He is a jealous God.

It is no accident that we are commanded to worship the God of creation "who made heaven and earth, the sea and the springs of water." Our generation has shown great contempt for God our Creator. First, we by nature resent a God who made us by His own will and created humankind from dust (Gen. 2:7; Ps. 103:14). Second, many resent that we were created male and female and that heterosexual monogamous marriage was His way of populating the earth (Gen. 1:27). This is an implicit way of bringing us to affirm the Bible; otherwise, how would we know about God the Creator?

## JUDGMENT AND THE FRINGE BENEFITS

I am not prepared to explain the full meaning of the words "The hour of his judgment has come" (Rev. 14:7), but it obviously points to the fact and truth of God's justice. "For the LORD is a God of justice" (Isa. 30:18). Those who have been saved must never forget that it is the gospel alone that prepares us for God's final judgment. It is appointed for all people once to die but "after that comes judgment" (Heb. 9:27). Whereas the gospel changes lives, gives us peace, shows us how our needs are supplied, enables us to enjoy God's guidance and providence, points to the way to live our lives, and lets us enjoy Jesus as a friend and brother, the main reason God sent His Son to die was to change our final destiny.

The gospel is preached to us that we *not perish but have eternal life* (John 3:16). It is my opinion that the passage in Revelation 14:7 shows what the gospel is like when it is proclaimed with great power. A sense of the fear and awe of God should accompany the preaching and reception of the gospel. I am sure it is what the gospel will do when the cry in the middle of the night awakens the church just before the second coming of Jesus (Matt. 25:6).

To put it another way, the gospel has fringe benefits: the privilege of prayer, the Bible, the promise of the Spirit in power, the gifts of the Spirit, the possibility of the healing of our bodies, and the privilege of casting all our anxiety on God (1 Pet. 5:7). But fringe benefits they are. The main benefit of the gospel is to get us ready for eternity: to be ready for the judgment that follows dying.

This is why a sinner's prayer would be, "God, be merciful to me, a sinner!" (Luke 18:13). We ask for mercy when we have no bargaining power. My own suggested prayer for one coming to Jesus is that they include the words: "I am sorry for my sins; wash my sins by Your blood."

The gospel is mainly about judgment and the fact that receiving the gospel prepares one for the judgment to come.

The judgment seat of Christ (2 Cor. 5:10) has two dimensions: (1) Christ the righteous judge will determine whether a person is saved or lost; and (2) the saved person will be judged by the Lord Jesus Christ—that is, whether one will receive a reward or be saved by fire (1 Cor. 3:14–15).

The person who receives a reward, having come into their inheritance on earth by their unashamed yet quiet honor of God, will receive Christ's "well done." It doesn't get better than that! Don't expect them to be among the famous we may have heard of. I believe Graham Kendrick got it exactly right. He said the superstars in heaven will be people we were never aware of here on earth. It is like those described in Hebrews 11. Many of those men and women referred to in Hebrews 11 did not get vindication in their own day. It came after they died. You and I must expect this. I dare say that I have very likely described *you*, dear reader. If vindication comes here below, good. If not, what is coming is worth waiting for.

What strikes me most about John's revelation of the

"eternal gospel" is this: the Book of Revelation was written between AD 90 and 100, some sixty or seventy years after Jesus' resurrection. The synoptic Gospels (Matthew, Mark, and Luke) had possibly been written between AD 50 and 70. Many scholars now believe that the Gospel of John was written before AD 70. In any case, the *last word* to refer to the gospel in the Bible is in Revelation 14:6. It is called the "eternal" or "everlasting" gospel. Is it different from the gospel in the synoptics? No. Or different from Paul's teaching? No.

My point is this. If the "eternal" gospel requires that we "fear God," this was equally true of the gospel throughout the New Testament. This further explains why people were "astonished" at Jesus' teaching (Matt. 7:28; 22:33). It also demonstrates that the gospel we preach should do the same today—leave people with a sense of awe. It is noteworthy too that Jesus could astonish people by His *teaching* as easily as He did with miracles (Luke 8:56; 9:43). I think many of us tend to think it will only be miracles that astonish people. This may be true. Peter said that "whoever speaks" should do so "as one who speaks oracles of God" (1 Pet. 4:11). Therefore, if God were to grant us power and authority to speak as we should, I suspect people would be virtually as amazed from hearing the gospel as seeing a miracle.

CHAPTER 2

# The Origin of Fear

I was afraid…

—GENESIS 3:10

Fear doesn't exist anywhere except in the mind.
—DALE CARNEGIE (1888–1955)

THERE ARE ESSENTIALLY three kinds of fear. First, the good kind—the fear of God. This is productive fear; it leads to peace, true knowledge, and wisdom. Second, the bad kind—the fear of man. This is fear that focuses on what people think rather than what God thinks. With one possible exception, which we will examine below, the fear of man leads to counterproductive anxiety, depression, and failure. Third, the ugly kind—satanic fear, which is supernatural. If not recognized and rejected, satanic fear leads to oppression, sometimes demon possession, and possibly premature death.

The fear of God is the sense of awe that makes one *feel* how real God is. The fear of God leads to the conscious resolve not to displease Him. To fear God is the beginning of wisdom (Prov. 9:10).

31

## FEELING

We need to grasp as soon as possible that we are not dealing merely with a cerebral, detached, unfeeling, intellectual, or unemotional matter. I have lived with people who are notoriously stiff upper lipped and seem to take pride in their ability not to show their emotions. For example, the Special Air Forces in Great Britain live by a rule: "Never complain, never explain, never apologize." I suspect living like this can lead some people to live in constant denial; it is called repression. Repression is consciously or unconsciously suppressing a thought or desire in oneself to deny reality. It is forcing the mind not to express feelings—for example, anger, disappointment, or fear. Repression is almost never a good thing. You don't really get rid of what you want to repress. You can push it into the cellar, but it comes out in the attic— as in high blood pressure, sickness, irritability, or even mental illness.

Take the issue of total forgiveness. We must not repress when we have been maligned and then keep no record of wrongs (1 Cor. 13:5). This is not living in denial of what they did. Not keeping a record does not mean pretending there were no wrongs committed! True forgiveness therefore is *not* living in denial that what they did was horrible. Keeping no record of wrongs is consciously admitting to yourself that what they did *was* truly wrong, but at the same time you also *forgive* by refusing to "keep a record" of it. That means you never throw it up to the person you have forgiven. In other words, total forgiveness is simultaneously accepting the fact of the wickedness they did and letting the culpable person off the hook for what they did.

That is what God does. He forgives and forgets (Mic. 7:19) but doesn't forget what He forgave us for! "Forgetting" means refusing to throw up their sin. See Matthew 18:23–35, which shows perfectly that the one who forgives does not live in denial.

So too with dealing with the theme of this book. We must feel. What we feel in our gut. Honest instinct.

By the way, there will be no repression when Jesus is seen openly at His second coming. John summed it up this way:

> Behold, he is coming with the clouds, and every
> eye will see him, even those who pierced him, and
> all tribes of the earth will wail on account of him.
> Even so, Amen.
>
> —REVELATION 1:7

People *wailing*? Yes. That is what you and I will hear. This will emanate not from one or two who are terrified at the sight of Jesus; it will be millions. No one will repress. They will not be protecting their pride and sophistication from those around them. What people think won't matter then. When was the last time you heard the sound of a wail? As I look back, I can only recall hearing a wail once—when I was fifteen years old. It is a sound one never forgets. People might cry. They might sob aloud. You won't remember their sobs. But the pathos that erupts in a wail is a sound you won't

33

forget. I have a friend who was present in the fire station next to the elementary school where the parents of those six children awaited news of whether their own child was one of those shot in Newtown, Connecticut, on December 14, 2012. She said the sound of their wailing as they heard the horrible news was a sound she never wants to hear again. Repression is not in play when a person wails. A wail comes when there is no hope—ever.

We will see in more detail below that there are essentially two ways to understand the fear of the Lord: (1) to experience it unexpectedly and (2) to be taught it.

## THE FIRST REFERENCE TO FEAR

The first reference to fear in the Bible was after Adam and Eve sinned in the Garden of Eden. Their eyes were "opened," and knew they were naked. They sewed fig leaves and made themselves loincloths. They heard the "sound" of the Lord God walking in the garden. He called out to Adam, "Where are you?" Adam then replied, "I was *afraid*, because I was naked, and I hid myself" (Gen. 3:7–10, emphasis added).

Was this the fear of the Lord that Adam experienced? Yes. He was ashamed of what he had done. He did not want to face God. Adam was created with a free will, hence "able to sin," as St. Augustine (354–430) put it, but now, having sinned, Adam feared. He was afraid to face God; the fellowship he had with God was now broken. Nothing would ever be the same again. He had been told that death would set in if he ate of the forbidden fruit (Gen. 2:17). Adam's sin meant an irretrievable and irrevocable shift for the universe generally and humankind particularly. The sense of guilt Adam felt is impossible to describe. You may be sure it was a horrible feeling and far more than the shame Peter felt when he denied Jesus (Matt. 26:75).

## WE CANNOT MERELY PASS THE BUCK TO ADAM

And yet the one thing we must never—ever—forget is that you and I were Adam and Eve. Don't say, "That is what Adam did. I would never do that." Wrong. You would have. I would have. Adam and Eve were pre-fallen creatures that represent what all of us would have done. The same is true when it comes to the crucifixion of Jesus. Don't say, "That is what the Jews and the Romans did. I would never do that." Wrong. You would have. I would have.

It is self-righteousness that claims "I would not do what they did." It was the self-righteousness of the Pharisees that Jesus exposed. The Pharisees said, "If *we* had lived in the days of our fathers, we would not have taken part with them in shedding the blood of the prophets" (Matt. 23:30, emphasis added). Jesus categorically condemned them for such pompous thinking (vv. 31–36).

We cannot pass the buck to the first Adam; we cannot pass the buck to those involved in the crucifixion of Jesus.

That said, only the Holy Spirit can cause a person to see this. An intellectual consent to what is taught

35

regarding the way humankind is, is not enough for one to *feel* ashamed of his or her sins. The Holy Spirit alone can achieve this in you and me.

The first reference to fear in Holy Scripture then is the fear of God. It was not fear that was taught but unexpectedly experienced. It is what Adam *felt*. This reference to fear shows a conscious shame. Adam did not know what God was thinking or what God would say. Adam had fellowship before the fall of which no greater can be conceived. But the first thing God said was, "Who told you that you were naked?" This is interesting; it shows that Adam's and Eve's *consciousness* of nakedness came without being told they were naked. A sudden shift in their awareness set it. They had been created naked, but there was no shame. But when they disobeyed the word of the Lord, they knew fear without being taught it.

And yet, strange as it may seem, the *fear of man* was also made possible by their sin. They had no fear in their pre-fallen condition. They had free will. They gave names to all of the animals. They were told they could eat of every tree in the garden except the tree of the knowledge of good and evil. How long their post-creation and pre-fallen state lasted is not known. It is an interesting question but unprofitable speculation.

## GOD'S VERDICT

Fear therefore emerged—both the fear of the Lord and the fear of man—because Adam and Eve instinctively knew they were not right with God. And yet they might not have known at first that this was a good sign. It meant that a loving, forgiving God was on their case. But at the same time, they would have to accept God's verdict regarding what they did.

And what was that verdict? Guilty. What was the punishment? Death. First, the day they sinned is when *death* set in. A relevant phrase is *game changer*, sometimes defined as a newly introduced element or factor that changes an existing situation or activity in a significant way. How significant was the sin of Adam and Eve? They brought *sin* into the world—and "death through sin" (Rom. 5:12). Game changer? Yes. Death. God warned Adam, "In the day [Heb. *yom*] you eat of it [the tree of the knowledge of good and evil] you shall surely die" (Gen. 2:17). The Hebrew *yom* can mean "era"; in the era of Adam's life death set in. Everything changed: his physical condition and his spiritual condition. Nothing would ever be the same again. He died at the age of 930 (Gen. 5:5).

Another relevant term is *paradigm shift*: a fundamental change—new and different—replaces what had been normal. What they were created with—free will—was normal. But their legacy owing to their sin was that humankind would be born in sin and bondage. What they enjoyed—an unbroken relationship with God—was also forfeited. Not only that; Adam and Eve knew they would die one day. Death was not normal. It was new and different.

Relevant here are St. Augustine's famous four stages of man:

1. *Posse pecarre*—man was created "able to sin" (before the fall)

2. *Non posse non pecarre*—"not able not to sin" (humankind after the fall)

3. *Posse non pecarre*—"able not to sin" (a believer after regeneration)

4. *Non posse pecarre*—"not able to sin" (after glorification in heaven)

This is the foundation of our historic Christian faith. I'm afraid it has been largely lost. In my opinion it is the second stage above—"not able not to sin"—that has mostly been lost. Why is this so? I think it is because we all resent any thought of our not having free will. We resent the truth that we are born in bondage. It is our sinful condition that blinds us to this and lets us run fast to the notion of free will. And yet God stationed "the cherubim and a flaming sword" at the Garden of Eden that "turned every way to guard the way to the tree of life" (Gen. 3:24). It was God's way of saying, "From now on only those who are invited may enter." Since the fall of Adam and Eve, we need a special invitation to get back to fellowship with God. All are invited.

Are not all invited? Yes! But not all accept. Those who are lost can only blame themselves. And yet those who are saved can only thank God for making them thirsty.

If we may fast-forward from Genesis to the very end of the Bible—the end of the Book of Revelation—we see these words:

> The Spirit and the Bride say, "Come." And let the one who hears say, "Come." And let the one who is thirsty come; let the one who desires take the water of life without price.
>
> —Revelation 22:17

It is noteworthy that in the original Garden of Eden the cherubim kept us from entering into the garden. But in the final chapter of the Bible—in which the "tree of life" is mentioned (Rev. 22:2)—the invitation is to "whosoever will" (KJV).

That said, you may know the phrase "you can lead a horse to water but you cannot make him drink." The water of life is on offer to the whole world! But not all want to drink.

This is why Jesus said two times in John: no one can come to Me unless the Father who sent Me draws him (John 6:44, 65).

### FURTHER PUNISHMENT

A subsidiary punishment was given to Eve and Adam while in the Garden of Eden.

To Eve the Lord God said,

> I will surely multiply your pain in childbearing; in pain you shall bring forth children. Your

desire shall be contrary to your husband, but he shall rule over you.

—GENESIS 3:16

To Adam, He said,

Because you have listened to the voice of your wife and have eaten of the tree of which I commanded you, "You shall not eat of it," cursed is the ground because of you; in pain you shall eat of it all the days of your life; thorns and thistles it shall bring forth for you; and you shall eat the plants of the field. By the sweat of your face you shall eat bread, till you return to the ground, for out of it you were taken; for you are dust, and to dust you shall return.

—GENESIS 3:17–19

To the serpent, also meaning Satan, God gave the first Messianic promise in the Bible:

I will put enmity between you and the woman, and between your offspring and her offspring; he shall bruise your head, and you shall bruise his heel.

—GENESIS 3:15

This was fulfilled on Good Friday when Jesus died on the cross. Satan saw himself as the architect of the crucifixion. Satan entered Judas Iscariot (John 13:2; Luke 22:3). Wicked hands delivered Jesus to the authorities. This is when the seed of Adam's "heel"—not his head—was bruised. He was bruised when they nailed in the nails. He was bruised by the verbal scoffing at the cross. But it was all part of God's foreknowledge and predestination (Acts 2:23; 4:28). And yet it was also the day when the *head* of Satan was crushed! Through Jesus' death the one who had the power of death was destroyed (Heb. 2:14). Indeed, had Satan and the "rulers of this age" known what was happening on Good Friday, "they would not have crucified the Lord of glory" (1 Cor. 2:8).

The only way a person can be brought to Jesus in saving faith, then, is by the Holy Spirit. Until the Spirit quickens us, we are all "dead" and in trespasses of sin (Eph. 2:1). A dead person cannot move. Cannot breathe. Cannot think, not to mention see their sin. The initial work of the Spirit, then, is to convince us of sin. By nature, you and I would never—ever—feel convicted or sorry for our sins. This is why Jesus said that the Holy Spirit would convince the world of "sin" (John 16:7–8). As Adam heard the sound of the Lord in the garden, so faith comes by "hearing" (Rom. 10:17).

Hearing comes by the word of God. It pleased God that those who believe would be saved by the "foolishness" of what is preached (1 Cor. 1:21).

Until the Holy Spirit came down on the 120 at Pentecost, none of the disciples knew why Jesus came. Or why He died. Even why He was raised from the dead. Even though they saw Him in the flesh after the resurrection. They did not understand the Sermon on the Mount. They did not understand the parables. None of this began to be clear until the Holy Spirit came down on them. Until then they sincerely believed that Jesus was the Messiah, *but* that He would restore the kingdom to Israel (Acts 1:6). And defeat Rome. All that Jesus taught about the kingdom being invisible went through one ear and out the other. Only the Holy Spirit enabled the 120 to see *why* Jesus came, *why* He taught as He did, *why* He died, and *why* He was raised from the dead.

This is true to this day. None of us can see the purpose in the gospel until the preaching of the Word—whatever the method—reaches our ears. It was the "sound" of the LORD God in the Garden of Eden that reached Adam and Eve in their sad state. Likewise, it is the hearing of the Word that saves us.

CHAPTER 3

# Understanding the Fear of God

The end of the matter; all has been heard. Fear God
and keep his commandments, for this is the whole
duty of man. For God will bring every deed into judgment, with every secret thing, whether good or evil.

—ECCLESIASTES 12:13–14

Come, O children, listen to me; I will
teach you the fear of the LORD.

—PSALM 34:11

Fear came upon every soul.

—ACTS 2:43

The concept of the fear of the Lord is the single most
important missing element in the church of our day.

—O. S. HAWKINS

THE THREE THOUSAND people who were converted
on the day of Pentecost were Jews. They grew up
with the *teaching* of the fear of the Lord. It was a concept

introduced thousands of years before. It emerged in the Garden of Eden. That Enoch "pleased God" before being taken to heaven would have meant that he feared the Lord. Noah moved with "reverent fear" ("holy fear"—Heb. 11:7, NIV) in building the ark. The fear of God was experienced by the patriarchs. It was a teaching enforced by Moses. It was an essential ingredient in the Psalms and the Book of Proverbs, and it was mentioned repeatedly by the prophets. Those people converted on the day of Pentecost would have learned about the fear of the Lord in the synagogues. Whether they ever *felt* the fear of the Lord for themselves before that day, who knows? But one thing is for certain. An immediate fallout of Pentecost was that "awe" (Gr. *phobos*—fear); it was very, very real to them.

> Fear came upon every soul.
>
> —ACTS 2:43

There are basically two ways one comes to understand the fear of God: it is either taught (through instruction) or caught (by firsthand experience).

As we saw above, the first time the fear of the Lord was experienced was when Adam and Eve were afraid in the Garden of Eden. It was not taught but caught. There had been no word from the Lord God that said: "Fear Me." There was no instruction about the fear of the Lord or a warning against the fear of man as in Proverbs 29:25. There was no caution about Satan showing up as an angel of light (2 Cor. 11:14) or resisting the devil

(Jas. 4:7; 1 Pet. 5:8). The fear of God that Adam and Eve experienced came not from teaching but by passively and unexpectedly *feeling* it after they disobeyed the Lord.

Fear is an emotion. It is what one *feels*. And yet it can be *taught*. Abraham is an example. He did not have Moses to spoon-feed the Moral Law. We have no evidence that Abraham had been explicitly taught the fear of the Lord, but he obviously imbibed it at some stage. He said to Abimelech that "there is no fear of God at all in this place" (Gen. 20:11). How did he come to think such a thing? The answer almost certainly is that by following and obeying the Lord, as recorded in Genesis 15:1–4, he developed a genuine fear of God. When he tried to offer his son Isaac as a sacrifice—but was stopped—the Lord said to Abraham, "Now I know that you fear God" (Gen. 22:12). Where did he get the fear of the Lord? Answer: it was in some way taught to Abraham as he listened to and followed the Lord.

Some things we learn by unconscious mediation. Some things can be mediated to us through our parents or peers. For example, how did I learn to speak with a Kentucky accent? Did I go to school and get instruction in how to speak as I did? No. It was the only kind of speaking I heard for many years. How did I learn to like classical music? Most Kentuckians like country music or bluegrass music. My mother, raised in Illinois, was a pianist and taught me to love Rachmaninoff and Grieg because she preferred this kind of music. Why did I want to be a man of prayer when still a teenager? My first memory was seeing my father on his knees every morning before he went to work. I found out that the most powerful preachers were men of prayer. Why did I develop the fear of God from childhood? It was because the fear of the Lord permeated the atmosphere where we attended church.

Therefore, the fear of God can be taught. But not necessarily by cerebral instruction. Otherwise, why would David say, "I will teach you the fear of the LORD" (Ps. 34:11)? How did he teach the fear of God? Simply read the rest of that psalm, beginning at Psalm 34:12. And keep on reading. Yes, perhaps you the reader could stop and turn to Psalm 34:11 and read the rest of the chapter. How do you come to understand the fear of the Lord? The answer is this: get to know God's ways.

The founder of the Church of the Nazarene was Phineas Bresee (1838–1915). He was known in his last days for going from one church to another with a most unusual message: "Keep the glory down."[1] Glory here might be defined as the manifest presence of God. For example, so powerful was God's presence that it became common that people who came to mock were unexpectedly converted. Bresee knew that early Nazarenes had no money people, no intellectual or high-powered people that would keep them going and expanding. Their only hope of survival: the glory of God. They experienced great joy but also the fear of God.

## THE FEAR OF THE LORD
## BEING TAUGHT

This is why the teaching of the fear of God was so important in ancient Israel.

You shall fear your God: I am the LORD.
—LEVITICUS 19:14, 32; 25:17

Gather the people to me, that I may let them hear my words, so that they may learn to fear me all the days that they live on the earth, and that they may teach their children so.
—DEUTERONOMY 4:10

And he said to the people of Israel, "When your children ask their fathers in times to come, 'What do these stones mean?' then you shall let your children know, 'Israel passed over this Jordan on dry ground.' For the LORD your God dried up the waters of the Jordan for you until you passed over, as the LORD your God did to the Red Sea, which he dried up for us until we passed over, so that all the people of the earth may know the hand of the LORD is mighty, that you may fear the LORD your God forever."
—JOSHUA 4:21–24

Serve the LORD with fear, and rejoice with trembling.
—PSALM 2:11

The fear of the LORD is clean, enduring forever.
—PSALM 19:9

The friendship of the LORD is for those who fear him.

—PSALM 25:14

The LORD shows compassion to those who fear him.

—PSALM 103:13

He fulfills the desire of those who fear him.

—PSALM 145:19

The LORD takes pleasure in those who fear him.

—PSALM 147:11

The fear of the LORD is the beginning of knowledge.

—PROVERBS 1:7

The fear of the LORD is hatred of evil.

—PROVERBS 8:13

The fear of the LORD is the beginning of wisdom, and the knowledge of the Holy One is insight.

—PROVERBS 9:10

Get wisdom, and whatever you get, get insight. Prize her highly, and she will exalt you; she will honor you if you embrace her. She will place on your head a graceful garland: she will bestow on you a beautiful crown.

—PROVERBS 4:7–9

Better is little with the fear of the LORD than great treasure and trouble with it.

—PROVERBS 15:16

The fear of the LORD is Zion's treasure.

—ISAIAH 33:6

But for you who fear my name, the sun of righteousness shall rise with healing in its wings. You shall go out leaping like calves from the stall. And you shall tread down the wicked, for they will be ashes under the soles of your feet, on the day when I act, says the LORD of hosts.

—MALACHI 4:2–3

## THE FEAR OF THE LORD BEING CAUGHT

Strange as it may seem, one of the earliest references in the Bible to the fear of God being caught—that is, felt and experienced—refers not to those who are a part of the covenant of God but rather those outside of it. And yet this was owing entirely to Abraham's presence. When Abraham went to Egypt and lied about Sarah, referring to her as his sister, it was because he hastily assumed that there was "no fear of God at all in this place" (Gen. 20:11). But it turned out that "God came to Abimelech [king of Gerar] in a dream" to warn him that Sarah was not only Abraham's wife but that Abraham was a "prophet" (Gen. 20:3, 7). The fear of God was indeed there *but only because of Abraham being there.* Consequently Abimelech, having experienced the fear of God, provided Abraham with great gifts (Gen. 20:14–18).

The second reference to the fear of God being caught is similar to the previous story. It happened to those outside the family of God! Jacob gathered his own family

49

and said, "Put away the foreign gods that are among you and purify yourselves and change your garments." They gave Jacob all the foreign gods they had, and Jacob buried them. As they journeyed toward Bethel, "a terror from God fell upon the cities that were around them, so that they did not pursue the sons of Jacob" (Gen. 35:2, 4–5).

Imagine that! As the presence of Abraham in Egypt caused King Abimelech to fear God, so the presence of the children of Israel did this to surrounding cities several years later. In the former account, Abraham had to come clean and admit he had lied about Sarah. Jacob likewise ordered his family to come clean and get rid of false gods that were utterly out of place for the covenant people of God.

I see these two stories as examples we need to follow today. There is no fear of God in the nation. There is no fear of God in the church. The world thumbs their noses at the church or at anything sacred. Legalized abortions for any reason are ever-increasing. And the people of God do nothing. Racism is still rampant in many churches. Same-sex marriage is now taken for granted. Theological liberalism prevails in many pulpits. There is no shame, no sense of disgrace, no repentance! I am convinced that if we today get right with God and become people of God who return to the fear of God, the world will be compelled to bow to the God of the Bible.

Just before God's giving of the Ten Commandments,

the people of God needed to get ready for this historic occasion. God said to Moses, "I am coming to you in a thick cloud, that the people may hear when I speak with you" (Exod. 19:9). There followed a thick cloud on the mountain and a very loud trumpet blast so that "all the people in the camp trembled" (Exod. 19:16). When all the people saw the flashes of lightning and the mountain smoking and heard the thunder and the sound of the trumpet, "the people were afraid and trembled" (Exod. 19:18–19). "You were afraid because of the fire," Moses said to the children of Israel (Deut. 5:5). Moses himself trembled with fear (Heb. 12:21). This was the fear of God that was caught. Experienced. Real. Paradoxically, Moses said to the people, "Do not fear, for God has come to test you, that the fear of him may be before you, that you may not sin" (Exod. 20:20). In other words, the experience of fearing God had a purpose—that the people not sin.

The fear of God that is caught is given not merely for us to see the majesty of God; it has a purpose, namely, to change lives.

Jeremiah promised that the fear of God would result in simultaneous experience and instruction:

> They shall be my people, and I will be their God. I will give them one heart and one way, that they may fear me forever, for their own good and the good of their children after them. I will make with them an everlasting covenant, that I will not turn away from doing good to them. And I will put the

fear of me in their hearts, that they may not turn from me.

—JEREMIAH 32:38–40

## GOD'S WAYS

God lamented of ancient Israel: "They have not known my ways" (Heb. 3:10). What angered God in particular was that the majority of the spies who investigated the Promised Land won out over Joshua and Caleb and did not go into Canaan *when they could have* (Num. 14:1–10). God has *ways*. You have your ways. I have mine. My wife knows my ways. I know her ways. You may not like God's ways! For example, He is a jealous God (Deut. 5:9). That is what lay at the heart of the issue with ancient Israel and with many today. Sadly, some hate this truth about God. He is a God of glory (Acts 7:2). He is sovereign, as He said to Moses: "I will have mercy on whom I will have mercy" (Exod. 33:19). He is a holy God (1 Pet. 1:16). He is all-powerful (Jer. 32:27). God wants us to love and worship Him for the way He *is*.

The Holy Spirit—the third person of the Trinity—has His ways. He can be grieved (Eph. 4:30); He is a very sensitive person. The chief way we grieve the Spirit is, almost certainly, by "bitterness" and unforgiveness (Eph. 4:31–32). The Holy Spirit may be quenched (1 Thess. 5:19); this can be done by not recognizing and affirming the way He may choose to manifest His presence. The Holy Spirit can be resisted, as when the Jews rejected the preaching of Stephen (Acts 7:51). The Holy Spirit can be blasphemed by people who attribute to Jesus "an unclean spirit" and thus are guilty of an "eternal sin" (Mark 3:29–30).

Jesus Christ, God's eternal Son, is the "same yesterday and today and forever" (Heb. 13:8). Just as there are those who think that the God of the Old Testament and the God of the New Testament are different and not the same, some do not realize that the Jesus of the four Gospels and the Jesus revealed in the Book of Revelation is the *same Jesus*. First, Jesus never apologized for the God of the Old Testament (His Father); He mirrored God Almighty. "Whoever has seen me has seen the Father" (John 14:9). "I can do nothing on my own" (John 5:30), only what the Son "sees the Father doing" (John 5:19). The same Jesus who is "gentle and lowly in heart" (Matt. 11:29) has eyes "like a flame of fire" (Rev. 1:14). The "bruised reed" which Jesus would not break (Matt. 12:20) has feet "like burnished bronze" (Rev. 1:15).

The God of the Bible is eternal and independent of His creation: the one and only true God—the Creator of the universe, the author of Scripture, the God who sent His one and only Son into the world to die on a cross.

I plead with you, reader, get to know God's ways. Embrace them. Esteem them. Honor them. The result will be that the fear of God will be a part of you. Never—ever—apologize for the God of the Bible.

The children of Israel *should* have known God's ways. But they allowed *unbelief* to set in and missed their inheritance of entering into the Promised Land, called God's "rest" (Heb. 3:19; 4:1, 9–10). The result for them? Cowardice. The fear of man. Listening to one another rather than hearing God. Counterproductive anxiety. Ingratitude. Stubbornness. Unteachableness. Unfaithfulness. Deafness. Hence the word, "If you hear his voice" (Heb. 3:7). As long as you and I can *hear God's voice* it is a good sign that we can still enter into our inheritance! It means that God is not finished with us yet.

It is only a matter of time before we must make a choice: whether to accept or reject the fear of the Lord. The fear of the Lord is a choice. The writer of Proverbs envisaged a time when people would call upon God, but "I will not answer; they will seek me diligently but will not find me." Why? Because they "hated knowledge" and "*did not choose the fear of the LORD*" (Prov. 1:28–29, emphasis added).

The reason that the writer of Hebrews said, "If you hear his voice," is because the Christian Jews in the AD 60s were already becoming hard of hearing—"dull of hearing" (Heb. 5:11). The worst scenario—God forbid that this happen to you or me—is to become *stone deaf.* That is what lay behind those who, having been enlightened, having tasted of the word of God, shared in the Holy Spirit and the powers of the age to come, nonetheless chose not to obey and affirm God's ways: they *could not be renewed* again to repentance (Heb. 6:4–6).

Not to affirm God's ways is a no-joke thing. I pray it

does not happen to anyone reading this book. And yet it could happen to you or me.

I therefore ask you: Will you choose the fear of the Lord? Joshua exhorted, "Choose this day whom you will serve" (Josh. 24:15). You must choose between making the glory of God your priority and making praise from one another your priority (John 5:44). Total forgiveness is an act of the will: to let your enemy off the hook or make him or her pay. You must choose whether to affirm God's ways or choose a god whose ways resemble what you want God to be like.

The fear of the Lord is "clean" (Ps. 19:9). Pure. Rewarding. Good.

PART II

# The Bad–
# the Fear of Man

CHAPTER 4

# A Most Important Choice

For God gave us not a spirit of fear but of
power and love and self-control.

—2 TIMOTHY 1:7

The only thing to fear is fear itself.

—FRANKLIN D. ROOSEVELT (1882–1945)

ONE OF THE worst addictions on the planet is to be in bondage to what people think of us. It is relentless, painful, natural, and an easy vehicle for Satan to seize upon and terrorize us.

Yes, it is natural to be aware of what people think of us. It is the reason we comb our hair, dress with decency, and even aspire to success. According to Ecclesiastes 4:4, a verse that shook me deeply over thirty years ago, all success can be traced to wanting to make others feel jealous of us:

Then I saw that all toil and all skill in work come from a man's envy of his neighbor. This also is vanity and a striving after wind.

—ECCLESIASTES 4:4

And I saw that all toil and all achievement spring from one person's envy of another. This too is meaningless, a chasing after the wind.

—ECCLESIASTES 4:4, NIV

You may agree or disagree with Ecclesiastes 4:4. But I would suggest that you search your heart very carefully and see if it is not true of you that we all enjoy doing things and achieving things that will make people admire us—or even be a bit jealous of us! I will be candid and admit to why this verse sobered me. Whereas I truly thought—and still believe—God opened the door for me to go to Oxford University, why did I *choose* Oxford? It is because Oxford is widely regarded as number one all over the world. It is the Mayo Clinic of medicine. The Wimbledon of tennis. The Madison Square Garden of all sports arenas. I knew that a DPhil (*Oxon*) would cause many people to admire me more than they would have if I remained at my seminary in Louisville. And yet although I still believe that God was behind it, I was smitten—and still embarrassed—to see my naked ego and pride in it all.

Keep in mind Jeremiah 17:9, that the heart is "deceitful" and "incurably wicked"—who can know it? We tell ourselves that we know our hearts. But do we? The more we delve into our hearts the more we see it is like peeling the layers of an onion: that the heart truly is desperately wicked.

And yet there is an irony that must be considered. It shows how anxiety can be useful. Whereas fear is troublesome and negative, there are positive benefits to it, namely, to motivate us to get work done. To achieve a worthy goal. To succeed. This is why I said earlier that the fear of man may sometimes be a good thing.

However, one cannot appreciate the danger of the fear of man until we see even more and in greater understanding how the fear of God is connected.

### THE EMERGENCE OF "FEAR" IN THE BIBLE

We saw above that the first reference to *fear* in the Bible is when Adam confessed to being afraid of God. It was after Adam and Eve had sinned in the Garden of Eden. God called out to Adam, "Where are you?" Adam replied: "I heard the sound of you in the garden, and *I was afraid*, because I was naked, and I hid myself" (Gen. 3:9–10, emphasis added).

The sound of God. That is what produced the fear of God in Adam. God's sound. His speaking. His word. It is my prayer that the *sound of God* might accompany preaching in our day.

This fear came after Adam had sinned. Any fear of God that may have been instilled in him before the fall was not sufficient to keep him from eating of the forbidden fruit. Asking why God allowed sin in the first place is like asking why there is evil in the world. We will not know the answer to that question in this life. That said, a fear of God emerged very soon after Adam sinned.

## A DEFINITION OF SPIRITUALITY

We should all want this, namely, to know the fear of the Lord as soon as we grieve Him. I would define spirituality as *closing the time gap* between sin and repentance. Some dig in their heels and take years before they admit to sinning. Some take months. Some weeks. Some days. Some hours. Some seconds. How long does it take you to realize or admit that you sinned? Or that you got it wrong?

And yet this book is largely about fearing God *before* we sin—in order that we might not sin. The fear of God must be taught. "Come, O children, listen to me; I will teach you the fear of the Lord" (Ps. 34:11). "Confirm to your servant your promise, that you may be feared" (Ps. 119:38).

The first message of the New Testament relates to the fear of the Lord. It is what caused countless people to make their way from Jerusalem to the desert—a distance of twenty miles—in order to hear John the Baptist preach. Some walked. Some came on camels. Some on mules. They were eager to hear John preach. They were not looking for the latest gimmick. They did not come to be flattered. They were not looking for brilliance or cleverness. They were not looking for oratory or a carefully crafted phrase. There was something else that impelled them to travel this distance. It was to hear a clear word from God. It was to hear what would be the first message of the New Testament: "Who warned you to flee from the wrath to come?" (Matt. 3:7). This was not a seeker-friendly message. It was seeker unfriendly. The people were attracted to a message that would reveal the truth. In this case it was related to the fear of God.

It is noteworthy that John the Baptist addressed that question regarding the wrath to come particularly to the Sadducees and Pharisees that came to hear him (Matt. 3:7). Why did *they* come to hear John? Was it because they were enamored with John? Probably not. They feared that the populace, the common people, were getting too excited over John's preaching. They were not so much threatened by John as they were that the *people* would believe and spread John's teaching. This is because the teaching of John the Baptist, like the teaching of Jesus, was a severe challenge to the authority, prestige, and power of the Pharisees and Sadducees. They went to the Dead Sea to hear John not to be edified but because they were spies. They would report back to Jerusalem (John 1:19).

## VARIOUS KINDS OF FEAR

It is surprising that the first reference to the fear of man in the Bible is regarding animals being afraid of us. God said to Noah, "The fear of you and the dread of you shall be upon every beast of the earth and upon every bird of the heavens, upon everything that creeps on the ground and all the fish of the sea" (Gen. 9:2). All living creatures are afraid of us, and this is by God's decree. We may be afraid of some animals too, but they are afraid of us.

But why are we afraid? Why are we afraid at all? Why is there such a thing as fear? The English words like claustrophobia or hydrophobia come from the Greek *phobos*—fear, horror. Phobia is used to denote various kinds of fear.

Some of us are afraid of the dark. My own earliest fear came when I was two years old; I was afraid my parents forgot about me in the dark. We may be afraid of falling. There are countless phobias. The number one seems to be arachnophobia—the fear of spiders. Do you know the meaning of *hippopotomonstrosesquippedaliophobia*? It is (seriously) the fear of long words!

There are men who have gynophobia—the fear of women. There are some women who have androphobia—the fear of men. But that is not what this book is about. This book is about the fear of God—which I call good fear—and the fear of people—which I call bad fear. What people think. What they can do.

## THE FEAR OF MAN: FEAR OF BEING HURT BY PEOPLE

The fear of man is not a rare psychological condition or trauma; it is the most common fear of all. The fear of man refers to being hurt, harmed, or humiliated by *people*. These come under at least five headings:

*The fear of physical harm*

We are given this promise:

> For he will deliver you from the snare of the fowler and from the deadly pestilence. He will cover you with his pinions, and under his wings you will find refuge; his faithfulness is a shield and buckler. You will not fear the terror of the night, nor the arrow that flies by day, nor the pestilence that stalks in darkness, nor the destruction that wastes at noonday.
>
> —PSALM 91:3–6

The fear of physical harm is more relevant today than ever. Especially for those who live in big cities. The violence that broke out after COVID-19 has spread all over America, and even to cities like London. In America it is the fear of being shot, in London the fear of being stabbed with a knife.

Included in this kind of fear is the fear of accident, fire, and theft. This is why many insurance policies pertain to fire and theft. When I drive in our car—or if our son TR is driving—I always pray for the blood of Jesus to be sprinkled on the car (and all that pertains to it) and the traffic (and all that pertains to it). I even lay my hand on the side of the aircraft when I walk on board a plane, literally praying for the blood of Jesus to protect the entire flight. I learned this from my friend

Charles Carrin, whose ministry consists largely of laying his hands on people when praying for them. I saw him do it, and I have done it myself ever since. I pray for the blood of Jesus to cover our condominium (even the entire building) to protect from fire and theft.

Psalm 91 is a psalm that every reader of this book should not only take seriously but (1) read often and (2) apply it, knowing that we serve the same God!

*The fear of one's reputation being damaged*

Let these words govern you:

> For am I now seeking the approval of man, or God? Or am I trying to please man? If I were still trying to please man, I would not be a servant of Christ.
>
> —GALATIANS 1:10

If you have read one or more of my books, you will know that John 5:44—quoted twice above already—has been my governing verse for many years:

> How can you believe, when you receive glory from one another and do not seek the glory that comes from the only God?
>
> —JOHN 5:44

I cannot tell you why that verse gripped me over sixty years ago. It may have come from the aforementioned sermon I heard at Trevecca in 1954 on Hebrews 11:5, about Enoch, who had this testimony before his translation that he "pleased God." I cannot say I have lived up to this standard—a very high one—but it has nonetheless been my chief measuring stick to estimate whether I might be pleasing God. For example, I do my best to make *all decisions* based on whether I please God—whether accepting or declining an invitation, writing a sermon or book, who I am seen with, how I answer a letter, or how I use money.

John 5:44 is the explanation as to why the Jews rejected Jesus. That is why Jesus put this question to them! He knew they did not believe in Him—and He knew why: they preferred the approval and honor of each other to the honor and praise of God. Paul knew this too. It is why he could say, "If I were still trying to please man, I would not be the servant of Christ" (Gal. 1:10).

*The fear of economic insecurity*
Jesus said:

> Do not be anxious about your life, what you will eat or what you will drink, nor about your body, what you will put on....But seek first the kingdom of God and his righteousness, and all these things will be added to you.
> —MATTHEW 6:25, 33

When I think of this passage in Matthew (taken from the Sermon on the Mount), I am reminded of two things. First, Matthew 6:33 was my dad's favorite verse in the Bible. He lived by seeking "first" the kingdom of God, knowing that "all these things"—food, shelter, clothing—will be added to you. The essentials of life are part of

67

the package when you seek first God's kingdom. As for my own father, he connected Matthew 6:33 to tithing. He was a strong and consistent tither. He believed that by living on 90 percent of one's income—and giving God His 10 percent—the 90 percent went as far as the 100 percent you started out with. He would also say, "Sometimes, son, I think it even goes farther."

The second thing that comes to mind regarding the passage in Matthew is a sermon I preached at Westminster Chapel many years ago and sent—with several other sermons—to India. My friend who sent these sermons reported back that the favorite sermon of all was on this passage. The sermon demonstrated that we did not need to worry about finances if we put God first. It apparently struck a note for the Christians in India. And yet I think this is a message that needs to be heeded by all Christians, wherever one lives.

### The fear of loneliness

> I am with you always, to the end of the age.
> —MATTHEW 28:20

> I will never leave you or forsake you.
> —HEBREWS 13:5

> At my first defense no one came to stand by me, but all deserted me.
> —2 TIMOTHY 4:16

One of the high-water marks of my time at Westminster Chapel was when Billy Graham preached for us. He chose "Loneliness" as his sermon title. It was an amazing sermon, one that helped wake me up to a problem that had not really got my attention. He explained how people who live in a large city are lonely. He described people who live in a bed-sitter who are lonely. This is to say nothing about those who lose a spouse, whether by death or divorce. This is to say nothing about losing a friend, whether by death or desertion. This is to say nothing about those who lose a cat or a dog—or a canary. I have gladly prayed for people who feared losing a pet. I have even prayed for the healing or survival of an animal that might be the only source of earthly comfort one has. Jesus at the right hand of God was tempted—tested—at all points like you and me, and sympathizes with those who feel lonely (Heb. 2:18; 4:15). You may laugh at one who prays for a pet, but Jesus wouldn't.

There is an old hymn that says, "How can I be lonely when I've Jesus only?" Answer: you can certainly *feel* lonely even though you have Jesus.

My mother died at the age of forty-three; I was seventeen. The loneliness I feared has carried over the last sixty-three years in which I have had Louise—but afraid I would lose her too. As of this writing I am eighty-six; she is eighty-two. I still have her.

My point is this. Are you lonely? I do sympathize. But Jesus does more so.

*The fear of failure*
  *It is right and biblical to pray for success.*

> Save us, we pray, O LORD! O LORD, we pray, give
> us success!
>
> —PSALM 118:25

> May he grant your heart's desire and fulfill all
> your plans!
>
> —PSALM 20:4

If I may return to my mention of Oxford, many people ask me, "Did you enjoy your time at Oxford?" The answer is no. This shocks people. But in my case it was and is the utter truth. Here is why: I feared failure from the first day I arrived at Oxford on September 1, 1973. I'm sorry, but this fear lasted nonstop until my oral exam on December 16, 1976. Please try to understand. I was born, raised, and educated in Kentucky. We were next to the bottom in terms of educational standards. Only Arkansas was beneath us. (We had a slogan, "Thank God for Arkansas.")

People have no idea how poorly educated I was back in Ashland, Kentucky. I was thrown in the deep end at Oxford, where the students were not only the brightest but also educated in the British system. Not only that, but I soon learned that 50 percent of the students who tried for the DPhil failed. One man who had been at the top of his class in Edinburgh University (earning what is known in Britain as a "first") failed. A friend of mine who already had a PhD from America failed to get the DPhil. I said to myself: "Whatever hope do I have?"

Louise was my great encourager. She persistently said that God would not make a way for us to go to

England if He were not going to help me have success in my academic pursuit. Her words were virtually my sole encouragement. Even the Lord Himself hid His face from me and gave me no internal witness that I would be successful.

But I made it. I was then invited to become the minister at Westminster Chapel. Now I was faced with following the greatest preacher in the world next to C. H. Spurgeon. I spent twenty-five years there, never once feeling the pulpit was mine. It was Dr. Martyn Lloyd-Jones'. I always felt like a failure next to him. I do not believe I failed. We had a good ministry. But I never felt successful when compared to previous ministers, such as G. Campbell Morgan and Dr. Lloyd-Jones.

Perhaps the most encouraging and motivating verse in the entire Bible is this:

> Delight yourself in the LORD, and he will give you the desires of your heart.
>
> —PSALM 37:4

My friend Josef Tson used to say that there are 366 admonitions of "fear not" (or its equivalent) in the Bible: one for every day of the year and one for leap year![1]

## THE FIRST REFERENCE TO THE FEAR OF MAN

The first account to being afraid was regarding Abraham. He took Sarai, his wife, with him to Egypt. Because she was beautiful, he feared that he would be killed. He told her to say, "You are my sister, that it may go well with me because of you, and that my life may be spared for your sake" (Gen. 12:13). Indeed, the Egyptians saw that she was beautiful and took her into Pharaoh's house. But the Lord afflicted Pharaoh and his house with great plagues. So Pharaoh called Abram (as he was then called) and said, "What is this you have done to me? Why did you not tell me that she was your wife?" (Gen. 12:18–20). So both were spared. This showed that God was with Abraham. God would have afflicted Pharaoh in any case; Abraham need not have made Sarah say she was his sister. As the psalmist would later say: "Do not fret—it only leads to evil" (Ps. 37:8, NIV).

The first reference to the fear of man in a person is found in Genesis 32:7. The passage records when Jacob feared his twin brother, Esau. Years before, Jacob had tricked Esau—the firstborn—of his birthright and later stole the patriarchal blessing of his father, Isaac. Esau had vowed to get vengeance: "I will kill my brother Jacob." That is what propelled Jacob to leave home. Years later, after Jacob had married and had many sons, he got word that Esau was coming to meet him. "I fear him," Jacob said (Gen. 32:11). Sometimes it is healthy to admit one's fear openly. Repression—whether it be a conscious or unconscious denial of truth—is almost never a good thing. It is best to face it. In any case this fear of Esau drove Jacob to seek God. He was greatly humbled:

> O God of my father Abraham and God of my father Isaac, O LORD...I am not worthy of the

least of all the deeds of steadfast love and all the faithfulness that you have shown to your servant.... Please deliver me from the hand of my brother, from the hand of Esau, for I fear him, that he may come and attack me.

—GENESIS 32:9–11

But there is more. The fear of Esau led Jacob to his greatest experience with God, when he wrestled with the angel and was given a new name—Israel:

Jacob was left alone. And a man wrestled with him until the breaking of the day. When the man saw that he did not prevail against Jacob, he touched his hip socket, and Jacob's hip was put out of joint as he wrestled with him. Then he said, "Let me go, for the day has broken." But Jacob said, "I will not let you go unless you bless me." And he said to him, "What is your name?" And he said, "Jacob." Then he said, "Your name shall no longer be called Jacob, but Israel, for you have striven with God and with men, and have prevailed."

—GENESIS 32:24–28

There is a fringe benefit to experiencing the fear of man. It is a snare, yes; it will surely get your eyes off God and cause you to disobey God's word. But it can also lead to seeking God.

Whenever God says, "Fear not," He is not referring to the fear of God; He is referring to the fear of man—the fear of losing your reputation by what people say or think; the fear of losing your job, your home, or your money.

## OTHER KINDS OF FEAR

David said, "The LORD is my light and my salvation; whom shall I fear?" (Ps. 27:1). Note: he does not say "what" shall I fear but "whom." This refers to people.

That said, though it is not the theme of this book, there is a fear apart from the fear of man, namely, *what* we might fear. The psalmist said we would be protected from the "snare of the fowler and from the deadly pestilence" (Ps. 91:3). A fowler refers to a person who uses a trap to ensnare wild fowl. It is not likely that many of us will have that to fear! But God assures us that the person who "dwells in the shelter of the Most High" and abides "in the shadow of the Almighty" is protected from all kinds of fear. I would assume an equivalent would be the fear of theft, a hurricane, a tornado, flooding, or fire. The "deadly pestilence" is elsewhere translated as a wasting or "deadly disease" (NLT). That could refer to cancer or COVID. I have been through several hurricanes. Was I not a bit scared during this time? Yes. Tornadoes come through our part of Tennessee all the time. Have I not known fear in times like these? Yes. Christians die of cancer and COVID. Most of us would have a fear of wild animals if in a forest, especially at night. Part of Jesus' temptation was being with "wild animals"—which must mean He was tested with a fear of them since the angels "ministered" to Him (Mark 1:13). In addition to these, there is the fear of war. One wishes that this fear would be eliminated forever. But it won't be—if only because Jesus said that the last days would be characterized by war and rumors of wars (Matt. 24:6).

Do we have an answer for those who may want to mention fear of things like this? John said that "perfect love casts out fear." Is this *all* kinds of fear? "Whoever fears is not perfected in love" (1 John 4:18). I think too of Psalm 112:7: "He is not afraid of bad news." Surely people are fearful of bad news. The psalmist envisages a person who is confident in God and refuses to be easily upset. The kind of fear to which John refers is with *people*—not accidents or disease. "Fear has to do with punishment" (1 John 4:18). John means that when we fear from not being perfected in love it is because we have bitterness and unforgiveness—and want to punish. Or we fear we will be punished. Perfect love casts out the fear that has to do with punishment to or from people. I believe also that God can and does give people a fearlessness in times of stress. I have experienced this, but not always. We may be given grace to rise above a tense situation—whether at night or when we are awaiting the outcome of an examination. I think God may do this in special situations.

Is there a difference between fearlessness and courage? Yes. Fearlessness is when you are not afraid. Courage is when you are afraid but make a valiant decision to do what duty calls for, which pleases God. Fearlessness is almost certainly a gift of the Holy Spirit that may be bestowed in a time of crisis. Were the Spirit to diminish, fear would return. Courage is when you make a decision to do what God calls you to do. It is an act of the will.

God does not require us to overcome the fear of disease, theft, wild animals, strong winds, or fire in order to please Him. I see Psalm 91:1—the benefits of dwelling in the shelter of the Most High—as a promise that God will take care of us in danger. This is why I pray for the blood of Jesus to cover our home, our car, and the plane I'm on when traveling.

We all have to die someday. We are not required to have the faith of God Himself (as in the Greek translation of Mark 11:22, "Have the faith of God") to please Him.

But when it comes to the fear of man—what people think—we are called to make a decision with courage, to resist being governed by what people think. In some cases there may be those who attain to *fearlessness* when it comes to the fear of man. Good. I want that. But I am not called to that. I am called to courage. That means saying no when it comes to the temptation to please people rather than God. As the fear of the Lord is a choice, so too is refusing to be governed by the fear of people.

That choice is what this book is about.

CHAPTER 5

# Why Is the Fear of Man a Snare?

Fear of man will prove to be a snare, but whoever trusts in the LORD is kept safe.

—PROVERBS 29:25 (NIV)

Fear your fear of man.

—MARSHALL SEGAL

THERE ARE TWO questions I will ask after I get to heaven (but not in this order): First, why was I a New York Yankees fan? In Ashland, Kentucky, all the people I knew were for the Cincinnati Reds. Second, why did John 5:44—"How can ye believe, which receive honour one of another, and seek not the honour that cometh from God only?" (KJV)—grip me in the embryonic phase of my ministry? It became the key verse by which I sought to be governed for over sixty-five years. All I know is that I was given a desire early on to please God and not man. I learned later that the fear of man is dangerous. The Bible says it is a snare.

77

Why is the fear of man a snare? Chiefly this: it is because your fear of what people will say about you can cause you to miss God's next step in your journey. It isn't worth it! But that is what the devil will make you focus on—your reputation.

There is nothing wrong with having a good reputation. After all, "A good name is to be chosen rather than great riches" (Prov. 22:1). "A good name is better than precious ointment" (Eccles. 7:1). But does not one get a good name by looking over their shoulder to discern what good and respectable people will say? No. "In the multitude of counselors there is safety," yes (Prov. 11:14, NKJV). Always seek good advice. But sometimes you have to make a final decision in solitude. "At my first defense no one came to stand by me, but all deserted me" (2 Tim. 4:16). If you are governed only by the opinions of people—even the best—when you know in your heart of hearts these people are not listening to God, following them and not God will cause you to end up with many regrets in life and possibly in burnout. A good name comes by seeking the praise of God rather than the praise of people (John 5:44). Live this way and you will have few, if any, serious regrets.

## WHAT IS A SNARE?

A snare is a trap. It catches you off guard—when you are looking the other way, or when you didn't think it could happen to you. It deceives. You are not likely to see it coming or you would avoid it. It catches you unawares.

You had no idea you were suddenly caught in a mess or that you were set up. A snare is what entangles. It is what stops you from moving on. It impedes success. It stops you from reaching your goal.

A snare is a trap used to catch birds or animals. The birds and animals you see in a zoo were caught this way. This is the way we catch fish. I am able to catch a fish because the fish does not know there is a hook in the worm when I am fishing in fresh water or in a shrimp when I am fishing in salt water. Artificial bait looks like the real thing to a fish, but it is a snare—a trap.

Because we are fallen creatures, we are vulnerable to a snare. A snare may catch you in different ways. For example, flattery. Criticism, which may demoralize. Money, which seems so right and good because you are in financial difficulty. Discouragement. Tiredness. Taking the easy way out. The shortest route. The road most traveled. The wide gate.

We *can* fall into a trap of our own making. It may be called "natural judgment"—you reap what you sow. Yes, it can be the devil, which we will examine below. For example, the failure to pray. The godly Joshua fell into the horrible trap set by the Gibeonites all because he did not take their proposition to God in prayer but negotiated with them on their terms right on the spot (Josh. 9:14–15). Israel paid dearly for it for generations.

> O what peace we often forfeit, O what needless
> pain we bear; all because we do not carry every-
> thing to God in prayer.
>
> —JOSEPH SCRIVEN (1819–1886)

Dear reader, how much do you pray? Backsliding begins in the knees.

We are vulnerable to a trap because we don't know God's Word. "My people are destroyed for lack of knowledge" (Hos. 4:6). We are commanded to "be ready to give an answer" for what we believe (1 Pet. 3:15). We are told to be able to handle the truth rightly (2 Tim. 2:15). One of my greatest concerns for the church at the present time is that people do not know their Bibles. When I started preaching in 1954 many laypeople knew their Bibles—backwards and forwards. Today, however, even many preachers don't know their Bibles.

I myself would never avoid tithing. It is not a guarantee to prosperity, but I have learned a lesson both from Scripture and experience: you cannot out-give the Lord. When I preached on tithing as a pastor there were those who understandably questioned my motives. But I am now retired and preach the importance of tithing all over the world. The only blessing I get from preaching on tithing is that I am consciously honoring God's Word.

We may find ourselves in poor health because we did not take care of our bodies. Overeating can cause diabetes. High blood pressure. Kidney disease. Smoking causes cancer. Sexual immorality causes syphilis or AIDS. Immoderate drinking can damage the liver. Lack of exercise can cause muscles to become weaker, and the result can be atrophy. "Use it or lose it," as the saying goes.

Applying biblical truth with common sense will enable us to avoid a snare—or see it coming and avoid it. The best way to deal with a crisis is to see it coming and avoid it. The best way to keep from falling into sin is to avoid the temptation you know you are vulnerable to. The sermon by the ancient preacher Ambrose (340–397) that converted St. Augustine of Hippo (354–430) was based on this text:

> The night is far gone; the day is at hand. So then let us cast off the works of darkness and put on the armor of light. Let us walk properly as in the day-time, not in orgies and drunkenness, not in sexual immorality and sensuality, not in quarreling and jealousy, but put on the Lord Jesus Christ, and make no provision for the flesh, to gratify its desires.
>
> —ROMANS 13:12–14

The devil can be the architect of a snare. He has a computer printout on our personalities, our strengths and weaknesses.

> The devil trembles when he sees
> The weakest saint upon his knees.
> —WILLIAM COWPER (1731–1800)

The devil has a way—under the protecting eyes of our heavenly Father—of tempting us according to our

81

weaknesses. He is somehow able to put a person in your path who will most easily and most quickly tempt you.

## INTELLECTUAL TEMPTATION

I once sought Francis Schaeffer (1912–1984), a great Christian apologist, for advice. He said something to me I have never forgotten: "Intellectual temptation is like sexual temptation; you never know how strong you will be." Some of us may be tempted to appear intellectual. Some may want to show how brilliant they are by appealing to people at an intellectual level. I was once tempted to go the philosophical route. By that I mean studying philosophy—Plato, Aristotle, Kant, existential philosophy. Francis Schaeffer's word sobered me, and I decided from that moment to stay with Scripture and be a simple Bible teacher.

But I came out of Oxford with another great temptation—to be a world-class theologian. My thesis at Oxford was not popular with many reformed ministers. I wanted to prove I had got it right in my thesis. But owing to the influence of Arthur Blessitt, I died a thousand deaths one Friday evening when I knew God wanted me to be a soul winner rather than a theologian. I have never looked back, and I have never been sorry. John 5:44 was what lay behind my decision.

For readers who do not know about him, Arthur Blessitt has carried a wooden cross (which he made) literally around the world. For more than fifty years he has walked across America, Canada, Europe, Asia, Africa,

Australia, South America, and every other land—even the smallest. He was listed in the *Guinness Book of World Records* for world's longest walk, approximately forty thousand miles! I predict there will be more people in heaven who were converted by a one-to-one with Arthur Blessitt than by any other person.

It is my opinion that most preachers, theological teachers, professors, churches, seminaries, Christian colleges, and Bible colleges go liberal for one reason: they want to appear intellectual. On the cutting edge. Not behind the times. To get respect from the world. It is sheer pride and the desire for the approval of man that lies behind this.

## TEMPTATION TO PLEASE PEOPLE

This is almost certainly our greatest temptation. If Dale Carnegie (1888–1955) was right—that the greatest urge in humankind is the desire to feel important—then our greatest temptation is likely to be to please people. And yet the irony is this. We will often be trying to please people who don't care! My Grandpa Kendall used to say, "Don't worry over what the other person is thinking; chances are he or she is not thinking about you at all." We are likewise prone to try to please people who don't care that much even if they do think of us. We are therefore not generally trying to please people who love us but those who may be jealous of us or even looking for a chance to say, "Gotcha!" when we mess up. Who can stand before jealousy? (Prov. 27:4). There is not a thing on this earth you can do to please people who are jealous of you. And yet foolishly we so often let their opinions govern us.

Peter wanted to please Jews more than any other group, so when Jews showed up as he was spending time with Gentiles, Peter hastily left the Gentiles for fear of the Jews (Gal. 2:12). Did he win the Jews over as a result? I doubt it. James rebuked the Christian Jews in Jerusalem for giving special favors to rich people who came to church (Jas. 2:1–6). Did he succeed? No. They drove them away and lost the poor too. A missionary couple left India to observe the Welsh revival (1903–1904) but was told by friends in London that it was all "Welsh emotionalism." Instead of going to Wales to see for themselves they returned to India rather than offend their friends.

Paul said, "For am I now seeking the approval of man, or of God? Or am I trying to please man? If I were still trying to please man, I would not be a servant of Christ" (Gal. 1:10). Yet when we speak of "pleasing man" it is a phrase that often means being motivated by the fear of man—that is, of people's disapproval. Their approval is worthless, but so many of us foolishly let it motivate us.

## TEMPTATION TO PROTECT YOUR REPUTATION

Whereas a good name is rather to be chosen than great riches (Prov. 22:1), and no sane human being will go out looking for a bad reputation, we can turn our reputation into an idol. The last words of 1 John are, "Little children, keep yourselves from idols" (1 John 5:21). An idol is not necessarily a wooden image or stone god that people can see. It is *anything* that might lure you away from desiring the honor and praise that comes from the only God.

I once persuaded a staunchly reformed friend—and fishing friend—to become a Southern Baptist. Not only that, but I recommended him to a church that later called him to be their pastor. He is now in heaven. But he never invited me to preach for him—or would even sell my books. Why? My reputation with most reformed pastors (who were not very fond of me) was more important to him than these men finding out that he was close to me!

Jesus did not think of His reputation when it came to those He chose, spent time with, or affirmed. Call it fearlessness or courage, you and I should be like this. When Billy Graham was criticized for being friendly with the Archbishop of Canterbury years ago, Billy replied, "He needs me."

## SEXUAL TEMPTATION

The devil often tempts by having someone flatter you. Generally speaking, women are tempted by flattery and touch, men by sight. But men are often easily tempted by flattery too. Satan knows exactly what will tempt you and the type of person that will appeal to you. Billy Graham said that the devil seems to get 75 percent of God's best people by sexual temptation.

Joseph, the favorite son of Jacob, forced to live in Egypt, could not have known that Potiphar's wife would be a trap. Neither did he know that God had earmarked him to be a future governor of Egypt. Joseph avoided falling into her snare—and became a hero of the centuries. What makes me admire Joseph the most is that he resisted sexual temptation when no one would likely find out if he slept with Mrs. Potiphar. She would not tell her husband. No one in Egypt would find out unless she told it. None of Joseph's family back in Canaan would ever find out. He may have thought to himself, "I don't deserve to be here. I've done nothing wrong. God allowed this situation to happen. He would understand it if I committed adultery in this case." None of these excuses would he come up with. His reason for refusing to sleep with her were (1) your husband trusts me and (2) God knows; "how then can I do this great wickedness and sin against God?" (Gen. 39:9). He had integrity and a desire to please God. And that was before the giving of the Ten Commandments!

I'm sorry, but Christian leaders are falling morally nowadays week by week. They also surmised they would not get caught. Adultery is a serious sin against God (1 Thess. 4:6) and does great harm to the church and its reputation. May I say a personal word to you, reader? If you are, as you read these lines, having an affair—or thinking about having an affair—please listen: *stop it*. Now. It is only a matter of time before you would give a thousand worlds to turn the clock back to this moment. Caution: "be sure your sin will find you out" (Num. 32:23).

God honored Joseph for his integrity and fear of God. *He will do this for you too.*

## FINANCIAL TEMPTATION

The love of money is a root of all kinds of evils. It is through this craving that some have wandered away from the faith and pierced themselves with many pangs.

—1 TIMOTHY 6:10

We don't know what caused Demas to fall. He seemed to be in good fellowship with Paul when Paul wrote Colossians (Col. 4:14). But something happened after that. We don't know if it was intellectual, sexual, or financial temptation—or what it was. But in Paul's last letter he said, sadly, "Demas, in love with this present world, has deserted me" (2 Tim. 4:10).

John described worldliness as "the desires of the flesh and the desires of the eyes and pride of life" (1 John 2:16). The pride of life is focusing on the here and now rather than eternity. It connects sooner or later to money. Yet it is not money that is the root of all evil; it is the *love* of money. We all need money. There is a sense in which "money is the answer to everything" (Eccles. 10:19). At the same time, one of the most alarming trends in our generation has been the emergence of the "health and wealth," "name it and claim it," and "believe it and receive it" emphases, especially on religious TV. This trend plays directly into people's love of money and greed. I would not want to be in the shoes of the people who have built their ministries on this sort of emphasis. As R. G. Lee (1886–1978) put it in his famous sermon, "Pay day, someday." These preachers will pay. Someday. This emphasis has not only left people theologically shallow but left them conceiving of a God who only mirrors their wishes. It is not the God of the Bible but the god they have projected upon the backdrop of the universe.

A Chinese pastor was given a tour of some American churches, all kinds. At the end of the tour he was asked, "What do you think of American Christianity?" He replied, "I am amazed at how much you accomplish without God."

The man I was named after, Dr. R. T. Williams, gave this counsel to ministers: "Beware of two things: money and sex. If a scandal breaks out in either of these, God may forgive you, but the people won't."

## A QUICK TEMPER

That's me. "Fools show their annoyance at once" (Prov. 12:16, NIV). I am ashamed to admit to you that I show myself a fool too often. This may surprise you, but all my life I have had this problem. The cause? Who knows—other than original sin. One of the most esteemed Christians in England said just before he died at the age of eighty-nine, "All my life I have had a problem controlling my temper. I never got over it. I still have it." Although this encouraged me a bit—misery loves company—I am still working on this. The devil is shrewd and knows exactly what will cause me to speak impatiently, whether to Louise, one of my children, or trying to make airline reservations over the phone.

I remember sitting next to Mrs. Martyn Lloyd-Jones at her ninetieth birthday party. A person across the room began to irritate me. Mrs. Lloyd-Jones sensed my anger, although I did not say a word. She whispered to me, "Take people as they are." She admitted to me that she once had a problem with her temper but got over it. I still hope to!

## LEARN NOT TO TRUST YOURSELF

We should perhaps fear these two things: (1) fear our fear of man because of what it will lead to and (2) fear the vast potential in our hearts to displease God. Here are three scriptures you should get to know intimately:

> The heart is deceitful above all things, and desperately sick; who can understand it?
> —JEREMIAH 17:9

> For I know that nothing good dwells in me, that is, in my flesh.
> —ROMANS 7:18

> If we say we have no sin, we deceive ourselves, and the truth is not in us.
> —1 JOHN 1:8

My Nazarene background sadly set me up to hope for the idea of sinless perfection. Most Nazarenes I know today would distance themselves from the notion of being sinlessly perfect. But that was not the case as I grew up. I prayed again and again and again—and again—to be sanctified wholly. The word "wholly" in 1 Thessalonians 5:23 (KJV) is what gave rise to the expression "entire sanctification." It was seen as an instantaneous spiritual crisis to be consciously experienced rather than a process that awaits glorification. The scripture 1 John 1:8 is what led me from believing I was sinless. If we "say" we have no sin, we deceive ourselves, said John. If we say that. I was taught to say that. To think it. But it was my baptism with the Holy Spirit that set me free to own 1 John 1:8. The experience of the Spirit led me to a sense of sin—and honesty.

When I discovered Jeremiah 17:9—that the heart is deceitful above all things and desperately wicked—I was at home. That was me. So too when Paul said, "In my flesh dwells no good thing." I could not help but see how the glory of the Lord led Isaiah to say, "Woe is me—I am undone" (Isa. 6:5).

The consequence of understanding human nature has been that I should never—ever—trust myself. That I should never take myself for granted, trusting that I would always perform well, say the right thing, make no mistakes, never put my foot in it, or utter the unguarded comment. After all, "If anyone does not stumble in what he says, he is a perfect man" (Jas. 3:2), having just said,

"We will stumble in many ways." Likewise, I know I am always a potential lover of praise, fearing criticism, hoping for compliments, and being judgmental of others. That is what Jeremiah means. It is what John means. What Paul means. This is why Paul could also say, "Let anyone who thinks he stands take heed lest he fall" (1 Cor. 10:12).

So I fear the fear of man. I feel so vulnerable. I am liable to be influenced by what people think or say and not focus on what God thinks or says.

For example, I preached for years thinking more about the theological approval of my hearers than winning the lost or encouraging the saints. There were people taking notes of my preaching and then writing books and articles about my teaching. It was not easy to dismiss people like this when they were present only to find fault. F. F. Bruce said there are two kinds of Scots: those who love to hear the gospel preached and those who come to see if the gospel was preached. That is what I have had to be emancipated from!

### EIGHT REASONS WHY THE FEAR OF MAN IS A SNARE

First, the fear of man will cause you to focus on everything but God. You say to yourself: "What will people say?" "What will my friends say?" "What will my enemy say?" This is one of the reasons why Paul said:

> Do not be anxious about anything, but in every-
> thing by prayer and supplication with thanks-
> giving let your requests be made known to God.
> —PHILIPPIANS 4:6

The fear of man is a signal to pray. And be thankful. To focus on God. To seek Him.

> I waited patiently for the LORD; he inclined to
> me and heard my cry. He drew me up from the
> pit of destruction, out of the miry bog, and set
> my feet upon a rock, making my steps secure. He
> put a new song in my mouth, a song of praise to
> our God.
> —PSALM 40:1–3

Remember to pray "with thanksgiving." When Jacob was scared to death he prayed; remember that he referred to God's "steadfast love and all the faithfulness that you have shown to your servant" (Gen. 32:10).

We are told to set our affection on things above, not on things of the earth (Col. 3:2). We are to keep our eyes on Jesus (Heb. 12:2).

Are you in a crisis?

> Turn your eyes upon Jesus, look full in His
> wonderful face,
> And the things of earth will grow strangely dim,
> In the light of His glory and grace.
> HELEN HOWARTH LEMMEL (1863–1961)[1]

Second, the fear of man is a snare because we overes-timate the value and benefit of what people can do for us.

> The LORD is on my side; I will not fear. What can man do to me? The LORD is on my side as my helper; I shall look in triumph on those who hate me. It is better to take refuge in the LORD than to trust in man. It is better to take refuge in the LORD than to trust in princes.
>
> —PSALM 118:6–9

Who might "princes" be if you are not in touch with the royal family? Answer: Those with money. People who are well connected. People you trust and admire. Authority figures. Or those whose connection with important people might advance you. Those whose recommendation you need.

If God raises up such people, fine. But make sure He does it!

The preacher Charles H. Spurgeon once said, "I looked at Christ, and the dove of peace filled my heart. I looked at the dove, and it flew away."[2] This is why we must always be looking to Jesus (Heb. 12:2). The "dove" in this case could be the person you think could help you. It could be the money you think you need. It could even be the answer to prayer you look for. I have lived long enough to testify that every person I ever began to admire too much sooner or later disappointed me. It is not their fault. It is my fault. I should focus on God not people—even the best. The best of men are men at best.

It isn't always easy. But one must focus on God and keep trusting Him. He will answer. He is never too late, never too early, but always *just on time*.

Third, the fear of man may cause you to overestimate the harm people might do to you. Louise and I endured several crises during our twenty-five years at Westminster Chapel. What made them so serious is that I feared I would lose my position as the minister. I feared that the people would not want me any longer. That public opinion would send us packing. What had happened convinced me that I was finished, that I had no future. When I was betrayed and decided to share my agony with my old friend Josef Tson, I assumed he would put his arm around me and say, "Get things out of your system." But he said, "RT, you must totally forgive them or you will be in chains."

What I thought to be the worst thing that ever happened to me turned out to be the best thing that ever happened to me! So too with every succeeding crisis. In each case I feared that the church would vote me out. Instead, they voted out my opposition. Some of these crises were satanic attacks, times when I saw firsthand how the devil always overreaches himself. Satanic attacks, as we will see further below, always result in the devil being defeated and openly shamed.

The devil tried to put focus on those who opposed me and make me think that my destiny was in their hands. Wrong! My destiny is in God's hands. God put me in Westminster Chapel without my raising a little finger. The principle of Galatians 3:3—what the Spirit begins the Spirit will accomplish—was at stake. God wasn't finished with me yet!

So too with you, dear reader. Are you in a crisis? Are you under an attack that is from the devil? Be of good courage! Satan is a defeated foe. His efforts are all non-starters. As the old axiom goes, "This too will pass." Romans 8:28 is true: "all things work together for good, for those who are called according to his purpose."

Fourth, the fear of man will make you take yourself too seriously. We saw how Abraham instructed his wife, Sarai, to tell the Egyptians that she was his sister. Abraham took himself very seriously indeed. He said to her, "Say you are my sister, that it *may go well with me* because of you" (Gen. 12:13, emphasis added). Abraham took himself seriously. He should have known better. He had been given one of the greatest promises in the entire Bible:

> I will make of you a great nation, and I will bless you and make your name great, so that you will be a blessing. I will bless those who bless you, and him who dishonors you I will curse.
>
> —GENESIS 12:2–3

When I first came to Westminster Chapel I took myself too seriously. I had just received the DPhil (*Oxon*) and wanted people to call me Dr. Kendall. I was afraid they did not respect me if they called me RT. It was my insecurity. I would be foolish to claim there is no insecurity left in me—of course there is, but I am a bit better in that department than I was! Call me RT.

Fifth, the fear of man will cause you to be less teachable and less open to criticism. The fear of man can make us defensive. Some people live defensively day and night. This means no freedom. But where the Spirit of the Lord is, there is freedom (2 Cor. 3:17). The result can be that we never learn anything anymore. It is as though we know everything and don't want to admit it when we are ignorant in some area.

We all tend to hate criticism. Somerset Maugham (1874–1965) wrote, "People ask you for criticism, but they only want praise."[3] So true. I'm that way. I send my manuscripts to friends for criticism but recoil if they criticize me. Yet I am more indebted to people's criticisms over my years than their praise. We don't learn much when people affirm what we have already said; we can learn a lot when they show us something we had not thought of. A friend of mine in England lovingly cautioned me on something I said only a couple of years ago. His words were life changing. It hurt a lot. But it was exactly what I needed.

Someone I did not know very well read the manuscript of my most recent book and said something that hit me between the eyes. What he said was so right, yet it embarrassed me so much. It totally changed my book. I ended up dedicating the book to him and his wife.

Sixth, the fear of man will keep you from being at home with yourself as you are. "Be yourself plus God," I used to hear people say. Why be yourself? Because that is the way God made you. He used your heredity and environment to make you as you are. You are wired in such a way that nobody is like you. God wants you to like yourself. If you say, "I hate myself," you slap your Creator in the face. He likes it when you like yourself.

One of the hardest things I ever had to do was be myself in the pulpit of Westminster Chapel. I was in awe of its history—especially following men like G. Campbell Morgan and Martyn Lloyd-Jones. I knew I was not like them and could never preach as well. I thought I must come up to the people's expectations and justify their choice of me.

The fear of man crippled me. How true: the fear of man is a snare. When I came to terms with the way God made me and that I had not asked to be their minister, eventually I was more and more like myself. I began to be the man in the pulpit that I was with friends. It was a good feeling. Oh yes, many—the same ones who did not like my reformed theology—criticized me for personal anecdotes. I recall something that President Harry S. Truman (1884–1972) used to say: "The person who tries to please everybody pleases nobody."

It is also true, of course, that he or she who tries to please God will not please everybody! But it is the best way to live, when you are truly true to yourself.

Seventh, the fear of man will keep you from being true to yourself. "To thine own self be true," said William Shakespeare (1564–1616).[4] That is not a biblical verse, but it certainly parallels Romans 14:19: "let us pursue what makes for peace." This includes inner peace—what you feel in your heart of hearts.

As I said earlier, when you are true to God you will

be true to yourself. God will never lead you to violate your conscience. The peace *with* God that comes from faith in Jesus' blood, not our works (Rom. 5:1), leads to the peace *of* God, which passes knowledge and understanding (Phil. 4:7).

Consider asking yourself, "Am I being true to myself?" when you are with certain people. When you adopt a certain set of beliefs. When you accept or refuse a particular invitation. When you go to a particular place. When you say what you say and do what you do. In other words, how do you *feel*? Our instincts are not put there for nothing. It is true that some—because of disobedience to God—develop a seared conscience. But that will never happen to the person who walks in the light of God (1 John 1:7).

The best and greatest decision I made during my twenty-five years in London (apart from Josef Tson's advice about total forgiveness) was inviting Arthur Blessitt to preach for us during the whole month of May 1982. Never in my life had I felt "fire in my bones" (Jer. 20:9) until then. When Arthur said to me, "If I agree to this, will you handcuff me or set me free?" I said, "I set you free." I knew it would be costly. It was. But the cost was worth all the turmoil, anxiety, and trouble that came from some of our deacons.

When you are true to yourself, you are free.

Eighth, the fear of man could keep you from fulfilling the will of God in your life. This is the bottom line of why we should not be governed by the fear of man. As

Paul said to Timothy, God has not given us a spirit of fear (2 Tim. 1:7). This fear is the devil's tool to scare you into doing what is against God's will.

I think Jacob got out of God's will for a while. This was evidenced in the way he reacted to his sons who took vengeance on the people who had defiled Dinah:

> You have brought trouble on me by making me stink to the inhabitants of the land, the Canaanites and the Perizzites. My numbers are few, and if they gather themselves against me and attack me, I shall be destroyed, both I and my household.
>
> —GENESIS 34:30

Jacob's reaction was out of the fear of man—what would now happen to him. But God stepped in and said to Jacob,

> Arise, go up to Bethel and dwell there. Make an altar there to the God who appeared to you when you fled from your brother Esau.
>
> —GENESIS 35:1

This was a pivotal moment in the life of Jacob. He got his sense of authority back. He said to his family,

> Put away the foreign gods that are among you and purify yourselves and change your garments. Then let us arise and go up to Bethel, so that I may make there an altar to the God who answers me in the day of my distress and has been with me wherever I have gone.
>
> —GENESIS 35:2–3

The family did this. Lo and behold, as they journeyed, "a terror from God fell upon the cities that were around them, so that they did not pursue the sons of Jacob" (Gen. 35:5).

This is what will happen when the church gets right with God! A fear of God will return.

Perhaps you need to go back to Bethel.

God has a will for your life. Satan will work overtime to get you to miss God's will. He will make things look "providential." He will use a person you admire but who could sometimes be an angel of light (2 Cor. 11:14). A person who has been generally wise could get it wrong—and cause you to miss what God is up to.

Here is an acrostic I have shared all over the world on how to know the will of God. Ask the following five questions:

- P. Is it providential? Does the door open easily, or do you have to knock it down?

- E. What would your enemy—the devil—want you to do? Do the opposite.

- A. Authority: What does the Bible say? If it is not scriptural, don't proceed.

- C. Confidence: Does it increase or diminish? It should increase if you are in God's will.

- E. Ease. What do you feel in your heart of hearts?

All five of the above just cohere. Not just one out of five or four out of five. But if *all five* of these come together, you have PEACE.

The opposite of the fear of God is the fear of man. Strangely, it is the fear of man that is responsible for keeping us from choosing the fear of God. The greatest competition in the entire universe might be said to be choosing the fear of man over the fear of God.

Yes, choosing. You must make a conscious choice. It is an act of the will. Don't wait for God to knock you down! When you see the evidence right before your eyes, proceed. If you don't have the evidence, *do nothing.*

Because people did not "*choose* the fear of the LORD" (Prov. 1:29, emphasis added), calamity followed. It does not need to happen. It does not need to happen to you.

An old mentor used to say to me, "We cannot get out of the will of God unless we want out." The God of the Bible is not in heaven waiting to say, "Gotcha!" He is not like that. He wants what is best for you. "No good thing" will He withhold from you when you desire to do His will (Ps. 84:11).

## CHAPTER 6

# How to Overcome
# the Fear of Man

Trust in the LORD with all your heart, and do not lean
on your own understanding. In all your ways acknowl-
edge him and he will make straight your paths.

—PROVERBS 3:5–6

The most dangerous person in the world
is someone who is not afraid to die.

—JOSEF TSON

WHEN I FIRST contemplated inviting Arthur Blessitt to preach for us at Westminster Chapel for
six Sunday evenings in a row, as I said, I had fire in
my bones. I truly had a taste of *fearlessness*—I was prepared to twist his arm to come regardless of the possible cost to my reputation and security as the minister
of Westminster Chapel. What enabled me to feel that
way? People have said they admired me for my courage.
But it was not courage; certainly, that is not the way I
saw it. It took courage *later*, yes, when I implemented

changes *after* Arthur's visit ended. But the initial thought of having him was born in an overwhelming determination that knew no fear.

Arthur initiated three things during his six weeks with us in April and May 1982. First, he gave a public evangelistic invitation for people to confess Christ. When he first said something about the invitation he would give, I said, "Arthur, we don't do that here." He replied, "We don't?" I then acquiesced, "Well, if you feel led, go ahead." He fired back, "I can tell you right now that I do." He did. It changed our history. Second, he got us singing contemporary songs as well as the old hymns. This was new and different for us. We kept it up. Third, he got as many as were willing to go out on the streets to present the gospel to passersby. This became known as our Pilot Light ministry.

During the week after Arthur's visit, I went back and forth in my mind whether to keep up what Arthur had started. I knew I could announce on the Sunday after he left, "Folks, we thank God for Arthur. But now we go back to business as usual." That would have taken no courage, and I could have avoided the greatest trial of my entire life—a trial that lasted almost four years. It was horrible.

The fear of man could be defined as *being governed by your perception of what people might say or do.* You imagine what could happen if someone blocks your plans by their influence. You feel that your destiny is in someone else's hands. The fear of man is the surrender of your autonomy, letting someone rob you of your convictions.

To overcome the fear of man is a remarkable accomplishment. But two things must be observed at this stage: (1) overcoming the fear of man may be temporary rather than permanent, and (2) there are degrees of fearlessness.

I mentioned the agony of the years that followed Arthur Blessitt's visit to us. It culminated in a church meeting. I remember it as if it were yesterday: January 16, 1985. My new assistant, Jon Bush, chaired the meeting as I watched. Six of our twelve deacons had decided to charge me with heresy. It backfired on them. But at the beginning of that evening church meeting it truly looked as though the church would side with these deacons. When all looked utterly bleak—at my lowest point, I had a vision of what looked like a pillar of fire, about twelve inches in diameter and four or five feet tall, at my right hand—I heard these words: "Lean not on your own understanding," from Proverbs 3:5.

Minutes later the tide turned and the church rejected the deacons' accusation. The six deacons were dismissed. It now meant that all I had sought to preserve from Arthur's ministry was safe and secure. Instead of our taking the next plane back to America to resume my old job of selling vacuum cleaners door to door, I stayed another seventeen years. We retired from the pastorate on February 1, 2002, staying at Westminster a total of twenty-five years.

Why did God give me that vision of a pillar of fire

with the words "Lean not on your own understanding"? After all, some ten minutes later the enemy was defeated. Why did I get this encouraging word? I would compare it to John 11:35; why did Jesus weep with Mary and Martha when He planned to raise Lazarus from the dead a few minutes later? I conclude: the Lord empathizes with us when we are at our lowest point even though He knows what will happen later. It is one of His gracious and tender ways. He wants us to know He feels what we feel (Heb. 3:1; 4:15).

As I look back, that vision of the pillar of fire plus hearing the words of Proverbs 3:5 prove that God was with me. But oddly enough, before that I never once received a witness of the Holy Spirit that He was on my side in the sense that He was for me and against them! There is a veiled hint in Psalm 56 that God may *sometimes* send a signal that He is for us and against our enemy:

> Record my misery; list my tears on your scroll—
> are they not in your record? Then my enemies
> will turn back when I call for help. By this I know
> that God is for me.
> —PSALM 56:8–9, NIV

David is saying that the defeat of his enemies proved that God was on his side. I might thereby conclude that our victory over the six defeated deacons shows that God was on my side and against them in that painful era. Yet I was never able to conclude that. Perhaps I should have. But these six deacons were respectable men. They had once been good friends. They loved my teaching. However, they could not abide Arthur Blessitt's ministry and influence on the chapel. The only way to stop what was happening—especially singing choruses—was to get rid of me. Yes, it was the chorus singing alongside the old hymns that these people mostly hated!

This brings me to my first point: how to overcome the fear of man. I need to confess that what I say next was not as clear to me forty years ago as it is now.

## WHEN WE ARE SOLD OUT
## TO THE GLORY OF GOD

Joshua was keen to know whether God was on his side or the side of the enemy. This came up when he saw an imposing, awesome figure all of a sudden after the Israelites crossed the Jordan and were waiting on a divine signal indicating what to do next. He saw a man standing before him with his drawn sword in his hand. Joshua went to him and asked, "Are you for us, or for our adversaries?" The reply: neither. "No; but I am the commander of the army of the LORD. Now I have come" (Josh. 5:13–14).

A story emerged from the days of America's Civil War that when someone asked President Abraham Lincoln (1809–1865), "Is God on our side or their side?" he replied: "What matters is whether we are on God's side."

Joshua was to learn one of the hardest lessons any of us must learn. Like it or not, *God is on His own side*; He exists for His own glory. Paramount in our understanding of the God of the Bible is this: He is a jealous God (Exod. 20:5). The natural man resents this about the true God. What we want by nature is a God who will do for us what we want Him to do—whenever we want it—to keep us happy. The notion of a God who has a will of His own is rejected by all of us—that is, until the Spirit of God changes us. This change, however, is what we keep on needing. Part of being changed from glory to glory is seeing afresh what brings glory to God.

Joshua would have known that the true God is a God of glory, a jealous God. Moses was his tutor. But now that Moses was gone and Joshua had no peer to turn to, he needed to discover God for himself—as if this were a new revelation. The sight of this stunning man—an angel—was going to be Joshua's next lesson in the principles of the glory of God.

One of my own earliest lessons came from my old mentor Dr. N. B. Magruder (1914–2005), who staggered me with this challenging statement: "My willingness to forsake any claim upon God is the only evidence that I have seen the divine glory." This means abandoning any sense of entitlement. We are living in the day of entitlement; people want their "rights." We transfer this to God, as if He owes us something. As long as you and I feel that God owes us something, it shows we have not come to love the true God— but only a god of our imagination.

Joshua may have thought God owed him assurance that He was on Israel's side. The truth is, God *was indeed* on Israel's side. But God deemed it more important *at that time* for Joshua to learn more about God than to be reassured that He was on Joshua's side. Sometimes God delays answering our prayers in order that we may learn more about His ways first. God lamented that the children of Israel did not know His "ways" (Heb. 3:10). Here is a principle I put to you that I guarantee will lead you safely throughout your lifetime: esteem God's ways as being more important than anything else you wish for.

Seeing the glory of God for yourself—not secondhand— will help eliminate the fear of man. You will be enamored with His glory, His will. The glory of God is the dignity of His will. Joshua needed to see this. It prepared him to conquer Jericho! Seeing the glory of God for yourself—that is, when you see how real He is—will enable you to stand alone and disregard the opinions of people. To put it another way: the glory of God is His own opinion. God has an opinion on everything; if you honor His opinion it is a guarantee that you will be safe and victorious in all you do! Wisdom is getting God's opinion—and honoring it.

Most relevant is Jesus' diagnosis of the Jews as to why they did not believe in Him and consequently missed their Messiah: "How can you believe, when you receive glory from one another and do not seek the glory that comes from the only God?" (John 5:44). When you *choose* the praise, honor, and glory that comes from God rather than the praise of people, you are in good stead—I would say brilliant stead—for what God will do for you in the future. Two things follow: (1) you learn you made the greatest choice you will ever make, and (2) you have found the best way to live.

It is better to lose your life than to waste it, as John Piper put it.[1] When you opt for the honor of God vis-à-vis the praise of man, it is losing your life. The promise of Jesus follows: when you lose your life for the gospel's sake, you find it; if you try to save it you will lose it (Mark 8:35).

The fear of man is basically selfish. We can be consumed with the fear of what people think about us, what they might do to us or say about us. But when you are fully, consciously on God's side—wanting only what He wants—fear is eventually removed. It leads you to perfect love, which casts out all fear (1 John 4:18).

Most of us have a question like this when we are thinking of obeying God's word: What's in it for us? We are in the "me" generation, as I said before. Consequently, too much Bible teaching today—whether in the pulpit or in Bible colleges and seminaries—basically puts this question in the back of our minds: What's in it for us? Most theology is anthropology, man centered. It is time to ask the question: What's in it for God?

When we become convicted and convinced that the proper question is "What's in it for God?"—and we find out what that is and follow through with it—the fear of man is on the way out.

## THE JOY OF PLEASING GOD

I was hugely influenced by a sermon I heard at Trevecca many years ago by Nazarene preacher C. B. Cox (1905–1976) on Hebrews 11:5, that Enoch—before his translation to heaven—had the testimony that he "pleased God." That sermon drove me to my knees like no sermon I had ever heard. It paved the way for the impact of John 5:44 (KJV) later—"How can ye believe, which receive honour one of another, and seek not the honour that cometh from God only?"—that would become my chief pursuit in life. Hebrews 11:5 does not say that Enoch pleased his friends. Or his parents. Or his wife. Or his enemies. He pleased God. God only. I do not have the vocabulary to unveil what the notion of pleasing God only did in my heart and mind that day.

When God answers prayer, He pleases us. When He supplies our need, He pleases us. When things are smooth and not rough for us, it is because God chooses to please us. We love it—and hopefully are thankful.

I put this question to you: Which gives you more satisfaction, when God is pleasing you or when you are pleasing God?

Is this an unfair question?

Of course, we all prefer for God to please us. Paul said he knows what it feels like to abound and also what it feels like to be abased, how to cope with plenty and how to be in need (Phil. 4:12). Which do you suppose Paul preferred? Easy answer: to have plenty, to be without want or in any pain. Of course!

111

But I put this challenge to you: learn to get your satisfaction from knowing you please God.

Let's back up. Do you *want* to please God? Would the knowledge that you please God thrill you? As we observed above, Enoch had the testimony before he was taken to heaven that he pleased God (Heb. 11:5). I would challenge you, dear reader, to get satisfaction more and more from pleasing Him.

You will ask: How can we *know* that we please God? Yes. It is by trusting Him when things around you are not what you want them to be. For example, some time ago I went through a period when nothing was going right—when I was low and feeling that God was certainly hiding His face. I was pleading with the Lord for a breakthrough when it suddenly came to me, "RT, you preach that people should get their satisfaction from knowing that they please God. Now is a time for you to practice what you preach by knowing you please the Lord at this very moment—*by accepting things as they are.*"

Hebrews 11:6 says that we please God by faith, that without faith it is impossible to please Him. That means when I keep my eyes focused on the Lord—and not circumstances around me—I may safely conclude I am pleasing the Lord! And when I see this, it gives me satisfaction. God knows everything I am thinking. He knows all that is going on around me. So when things are adverse, it is as if God is handing me the privilege of knowing I please Him on a silver platter.

My point is this. When I embrace the privilege of

pleasing God by sheer faith, and esteem pleasing Him more than pleasing people, the fear of man vanishes.

## THE FEAR OF CHASTENING

Chastening, being disciplined, is inevitable if you truly are a child of God. Whom the Lord loves He disciplines (Heb. 12:6). If we are without discipline, we are "illegitimate children" (Heb. 12:8). This means that a measure of chastening is going to come to you and me sooner or later; it is evidence that we really are saved.

That said, there are degrees of chastening and more than one reason that may lie behind chastening. First, chastening is essentially preparation, not God "getting even" because we sinned. God got even at the cross of Jesus Christ. The blood of Jesus satisfied God's wrath. So why does God chasten us? Because He is not finished with us yet. He has more work for us to do. We need correction. God wants us equal to the task He has in view for us. We go to school to learn. We are chastened in order to learn God's ways. As we have seen, God wants us to know His ways.

There are three kinds of chastening: internal chastening (God's plan A); external chastening (plan B); and terminal chastening (plan C). Internal chastening is carried out by the Holy Spirit as we read God's Word. That is the best way to have your problem solved! Read God's Word; obey sound teaching. That is God's plan A. But most of us need something external before God has our attention. God sent the wind and the big fish to deal with Jonah. Those in Corinth were "weak" and "sickly" from their abuse of fellow believers regarding the Lord's Supper (1 Cor. 11:30). When plan A does not work, God resorts to plan B, which will hopefully drive us to our knees and bring us to repentance. But some in Corinth actually died (1 Cor. 11:30). John calls it the sin that leads to death (1 John 5:16–17). This is terminal chastening.

Whereas chastening is essentially preparation because God is in the process of equipping us for service, sometimes God rolls up His sleeves and does what it takes to get our attention. He may put you on your back. It may be financial reverse. It could be the hiding of His face. There are a thousand ways God may choose to bring us to submission. God came to Jonah a "second time" (Jon. 3:1). But had not Jonah obeyed this time, God would carry out terminal chastening. I reckon too that terminal chastening is of two sorts: some die a premature death, and some live but are unable to repent (Heb. 6:4–6). Jacob's brother, Esau, could find no place of repentance though he sought it with tears (Heb. 12:17).

The purpose of chastening is to lead us to holiness (Heb. 12:10). Plan A can do it. Plan B may be necessary for us. Let us hope nobody reading this will experience plan C, terminal chastening. The end result will be salvation by fire (1 Cor. 3:14–15).

David was a man after God's own heart. But God is no respecter of persons. David's adultery and attempt to cover it up with murder led to severe punishment for him (2 Sam. 12). David was being disciplined by God, but it is also true that God was not finished with him. David repented and became a genuine man of God in his later years.

The fear of chastening is what keeps some of us on the straight and narrow. God can be rugged—even ruthless—with His own. Take sexual immorality, for example. Paul warned that "the Lord is an avenger" when it comes to His own children indulging in sexual sin (1 Thess. 4:3–7). Caution: "Be sure your sin will find you out" (Num. 32:23). Further caution: if you have sinned with a high hand—going willfully against explicit admonitions in Scripture—and have not been disciplined, it could mean it is because you are not a true child of God. I am not saying that you are not saved (I am not your judge). But it should be a sobering moment for you as you read these lines and admit you have got away with some pretty awful stuff. I will add one more thing: if you need this solemn word and have not been chastened, just maybe God will use *this very word now* to get your attention—actually using plan A in your case!

God uses the *fear* of chastening as well as chastening itself to get our attention.

And for what reason? That we will be duly convicted over the sin of the fear of man. God wants you to fear Him. Not people. He is a jealous God.

And yet "he knows our frame; he remembers that we are dust" (Ps. 103:14). He will not always chide. He knows each of us backward and forward. We all have this problem with the fear of man and experience the consequences of being manipulated by what people think. However, we still need to avoid the fear of man with all our hearts.

## LEARN TO ESCHEW COMPLIMENTS

We all love compliments. Every preacher loves compliments *immediately* following his sermon—from the great Dr. Martyn Lloyd-Jones to Dr. Billy Graham. My British friend Lyndon Bowring has a theory: never offer the slightest criticism to a preacher right after he or she just finished preaching. So true. We all want to know that we didn't mess up when we just preached. Lyndon says to wait a day or two if you have a suggestion to that preacher. (But I soon found I could not enjoy Lyndon's compliment after I preached, knowing I would get the truth later!)

The Nazarene preacher known as Uncle Buddy Robinson (1860–1942) told of how a person came up to him and said, "Uncle Buddy, that is the greatest sermon I ever heard," so he prayed: "Lord, don't let me get puffed up." Seconds later someone said to him, "Uncle Buddy, that is the worst sermon I ever heard." He prayed, "Lord, don't let me get puffed down."

I had the high privilege of being tutored by Dr. Lloyd-Jones every Thursday between 11:00 a.m. and 1 p.m. for the first four years I was at Westminster Chapel. He was gracious and gave me a compliment now and then when he felt I needed one, but he did not spare telling me what else I needed to hear during those years. The worst mistake I made during that time, however, was to let my mood swing according to the compliments of my hearers. It is not easy to disregard compliments.

But what I can offer is this: whether you are a preacher or a layperson, we can learn not to take compliments too seriously. Jesus said we should not let our right hand know what our left hand is doing when it comes to giving (Matt. 6:3), something that is almost impossible to do. But as John Stott put it, there is a sense in which *we do not even tell ourselves* when or what we have given. In other words, we must refuse to gloat over having given—whether tithing to a church or contributing to a charity. "Refuse to think about it," as Dr. Lloyd-Jones would say.

We must learn to do this with compliments, whether regarding the work we do, our appearance, or doing our duty. It is an intentional attempt to let what people say go through one ear and out the other. Don't dwell on it. And I would suggest this when you are complimented: pray from your heart, "Thank You, Lord, for this nice word; I give You the glory and ask that You help me to ignore it as best I can."

I begged God to compliment me one evening. I did. It was after preaching to two thousand people at the Easter People event thirty years ago in Bournemouth, England. No one complimented, neither the people who invited me nor anybody nearby. As I drove back to London, I said, "Lord, did I do okay?" Silence. Twenty years later as I was walking out of an Anglican church in Wembley, London, a lady stopped me and said: "I have been wanting to reach you for several years. Many years ago you preached for Easter People in Bournemouth, but you probably don't remember it."

"Oh, I remember it well," I assured the lady.

"I was converted that night," she added. That was pleasant to hear, but I had to admit that in my vanity I was not thinking about souls but rather how well I did. It was shameful.

God is a jealous God and is not pleased when we receive compliments from each other and make no attempt to seek the glory that comes from Him (John 5:44). As long as we thrive on praise, we will also be hypersensitive to what people think. The fear of man is a snare because it militates from seeking the honor that comes from the only God.

## COURAGE: AN ACT OF THE WILL

At the end of the day, none of us will be fully emancipated from the desire for compliments or the dislike of criticism.

So what do we do? We must have a rugged determination to do the right thing—what Graham Kendrick calls "a steely-eyed endurance" in his song "For This I Have Jesus." It is an act of the will. You must not wait for God to knock you down; you must do what you know in your heart of hearts God is requiring of you. This is the case with total forgiveness. You must decide in your heart to (1) not tell anyone what your enemy did or said to you or about you; (2) treat those who hurt you with tenderness and gentleness; (3) not wait for them to feel sorry for what they did (they probably never will); (4) let them save face (you cover for them and do not rub their faces in it); (5) protect them by never revealing what could be their darkest secret; (6) practice total forgiveness for the rest of your life—it is a life sentence; and (7) pray that God will bless them.

When you can sincerely pray that God will bless them—and even pray that God will not let them get found out—you are in a world of peace and joy. If God wants them to get found out, caught, or punished for their horrible attitude, He will do it. His way. And in His time. This is why God said, "Vengeance is mine" (Rom. 12:19). I can assure you that He does not want your help. Once you try to help Him punish that evil person, God will back off and let you have a go. I promise you things will get worse. And worse. Don't deprive God of doing what He does best, namely, to vindicate the truth and punish those who abuse it. Read the story of Esther and see how God vindicated Mordecai (Est. 3–10).

There is nothing like practicing total forgiveness from your heart when it comes to overcoming the fear of man. Not only that, but the greater the suffering the greater the anointing. The greater the injustice hurled at you, the greater the promise of blessing. If it were to be revealed that you have suffered more than all those around you, the angels would have a word for you: congratulations! You are in good stead for a blessing from the Holy Spirit that your friends don't have. Take the mistreatment with both hands! But don't complain and don't make too much of it, lest you feel entitled (as we will see below). I refer to setting free those people who have hurt you, those who wanted to destroy you, or those who have been unkind, abusive, or unfaithful to you—even if they were once close to you. Total forgiveness, when it comes to overcoming the fear of man, is the fastest track to internal freedom I know of. Totally forgiving an enemy has an amazing way of setting you free from being afraid of *all* people.

## DON'T EXPECT GOD TO BEND THE RULES FOR YOU

Always be ready to fight a feeling of entitlement. Entitlement is one of the curses of our day. In this "What's in it for me?" age, so many feel entitled, as if God owes them something. On top of that, when we do what is required of us—whether talking to others about Jesus or walking in total forgiveness—we must resist any feeling that we have done something wonderful.

The devil will try to make us feel special or the exception to the rule. He wants you to feel sorry for yourself. I have to tell you, I have learned the hard way: self-pity gets us nowhere. It doesn't work. It doesn't help. It doesn't score points with God.

Jesus spoke to this:

> Will any one of you who has a servant plowing or keeping sheep say to him when he has come in from the field, "Come at once and recline at

table"? Will he not rather say to him, "Prepare supper for me, and dress properly, and serve me while I eat and drink"? Does he thank the servant because he did what was commanded? So you also, when you have done all that you were commanded, say, "We are unworthy servants, we have only done our duty."

—LUKE 17:7–10

I remember coming in from a hard week of ministry, having slept poorly, in deep jet lag, and preaching many times in a few days, feeling tired. I am ashamed to say I had to fight a feeling of self-pity. Suddenly Luke 17:10 came to me, and I snapped out of it. I was only doing my duty! And it was an immense privilege. As we saw earlier, Joshua learned from the commander of the Lord's armies that God owed him *nothing*! God didn't bend the rules for Joshua. Or Moses. Or Samuel. If we have an ambition to follow in the train of those men and women described in Hebrews 11, it means that we must welcome our lot, dignify every trial, and be thankful for the privilege of doing our duty for the Most High God.

It is a supreme honor to work for the Lord. If you were assigned a duty by a head of state, a prime minister, or Her Majesty the Queen, would you not consider it a privilege? It doesn't get better than working for Jesus. Totally forgiving for Jesus. Getting tired for Jesus. Not sleeping well for Jesus. We are not our own; we are bought with a price.

## DELAY VINDICATION AND
## REWARD UNTIL THE JUDGMENT
## SEAT OF CHRIST

Do you know what it is to want vindication when you have been misunderstood? When you have been wrongly judged? When you have taken a stand for a principle no one else appreciated?

I have a theory: vindication at the judgment seat of Christ will be infinitely more satisfying and rewarding than having your name cleared here on earth. To receive a "well done" from our sovereign Redeemer will be more thrilling than any person saying here, "You were right." Who cares whether people think we are right? What is their approval worth?

My advice: don't raise a little finger to clear your name. Let God do it. His way. And in His time. Never forget the way Paul looked at this sort of thing:

> But with me it is a very small thing that I should be judged by you or by any human court. In fact, I don't even judge myself. For I am not aware of anything against myself, but I am not thereby acquitted. It is the Lord who judges me. Therefore do not pronounce judgment before the time before the Lord does, who will bring to light the things now hidden in darkness and will disclose the purpose of the heart. Then each one will receive his commendation from God.
>
> —1 CORINTHIANS 4:3–5

One day all things will be out in the open. There will be nothing hidden. "For nothing is hidden that will not be made manifest, nor is anything secret that will not be known and come to light" (Luke 8:17). We will then find out who was real—the real deal—who was pure gold, and who had transparent integrity. All phonies will be exposed. It will be a day worth waiting for.

As far as we know, Joseph was never vindicated, having been accused of sleeping with Potiphar's wife. He was made prime minister of Egypt because God was with him (Gen. 39:2, 21). God was also with Joseph to interpret Pharaoh's dreams. I have often wondered what Potiphar's wife thought (or what her husband must have thought) when Joseph was exalted as he was. Joseph tried to get the butler—or cupbearer to the king—to put in a good word for him to the pharaoh. But he forgot (Gen. 40:23). God had a better idea. God gets great glory when He alone exalts us, not when we pull strings, exploit our connections, or choose the best seat at a banquet (Luke 14:10). This is why Jesus told us to take the "lowest" seat—to wait on God's timing. He that exalts himself will be abased. He who humbles himself will be exalted (Luke 14:11).

God does the exalting that matters.

It is only a matter of time when all of us will be ashamed that we let the fear of man make our decisions for us. The people we fear will one day be shown to be cowards and people of great weakness and pity. We will be disgusted with ourselves that we ever let people influence us rather than get our self-esteem from God's approval.

I asked myself, who exactly have I possibly feared most in my lifetime that might do me harm? Not physical harm but that which might cause me to lose favor with those who once respected me. I have thought about this a lot. The answer almost certainly is that doors would close that had been open. Strange as it may seem, my critics have been among those I most agreed with theologically. They have nonetheless succeeded in closing open doors I might have had with reformed Evangelicals. Oddly enough, I have never had an unkind word come from a Pentecostal, a Charismatic, or an Arminian. I could write a book on the books and articles written against me by the reformed! Have they hurt me? It depends on how one interprets "hurt." If you mean have they made me feel bad? Yes. It has hurt a lot, my greatest emotional pain for sure. The disappointment of my life. But John 5:44 and 1 Corinthians 4:5 are what have preserved me.

I think Paul always wanted to reach his own people, the Jews. But God made it clear that Paul was directed to Gentiles (Gal. 2:9). I have wanted to reach the reformed. After all, I have (in my opinion) what they need—an openness to the Spirit. But God has largely closed doors to reach the very people I so wanted to be accepted by.

## WHEN YOU ARE UNAFRAID TO DIE

Josef Tson used to say to me again and again, "The most dangerous person in the world is one who is unafraid to die." This refers to good men and evil men. Consider the men who took over the controls on airplanes that went straight into the New York twin towers and the Pentagon on September 11, 2001. These men were fearless. They were totally dedicated to Islam, Allah, and hatred for America. They took courses on flying jet planes just to be prepared to do what they eventually did. September 11—a day that lives in infamy—was planned years in advance. The major qualification was being unafraid to die.

Jesus told Peter how he would die, by what death he was to glorify God:

> Truly, truly, I say to you, when you were young, you used to dress yourself and walk wherever you wanted, but when you are old, you will stretch out your hands, and another will dress you and carry you where you do not want to go.
>
> —JOHN 21:18

According to legend, as the authorities in Rome were intending to crucify Peter, the apostle asked that he be crucified upside down, for he was not worthy to be crucified the same way as his Lord. At about the same time, around AD 65, the apostle Paul was beheaded in Rome. In his last epistle Paul wrote

> I am already being poured out as a drink offering, and the time of my departure has come. I have fought the good fight, I have finished the race, I have kept the faith. Henceforth there is laid up for me the crown of righteousness, which the Lord,

125

the righteous judge, will award to me on that day, and not only to me but to all who have loved his appearing.

—2 TIMOTHY 4:6–8

The martyrs of the early church were unafraid to die. Ignatius, the bishop of Antioch (*d.* 108 BC), relished the thought of dying for Christ. A disciple of the apostle John, Ignatius urged all his friends not to stop the authorities from killing him. He wanted to be "ground by the teeth of the wild beasts" that he might be the "wheat of God." "I am only beginning to be a disciple," he said, at the thought of dying for Jesus.[2] His friend Polycarp, bishop of Smyrna (*d.* AD 150), was to be burnt at the stake. The authorities commanded him to praise Caesar and deny Christ. Polycarp replied, "Fourscore and six years have I served him, and he has never done me injury; how then can I now blaspheme my King and savior? Ignite the flame."[3] As the flames began to burn his body, a wind came into the stadium and caused the fire to encircle his body, and Polycarp would not die! Then they threw a spear into his side; the blood and water from his body extinguished the flame, and then he died.

Bishop Hugh Latimer (1485–1555) and Bishop Nicholas Ridley (1500–1555) died at the stake in the Balliol ditch in Oxford. They were tied back-to-back. As the flames began to come upon their bodies, Latimer shouted back at Ridley, "Play the man, Master Ridley; we shall this day light such a candle, by God's grace, in England, as I trust shall never be put out."[4] A year later Archbishop Thomas Cranmer (1489–1556) died at the stake in the same Balliol ditch at Oxford. He held out his hand directly into the flame—the hand that had signed his recantation regarding the Eucharist—of which he became ashamed. He wanted that hand to burn first. John Bradford (1510–1555), prebendary of St. Paul's Cathedral in London, was burned at the stake in Smithfield, London, with fellow-martyr John Leaf. His last words were: "Be of good comfort, brother; for we shall have a merry supper with the Lord this night!"[5]

I remember reading these accounts of the Marian martyrs, as they were called (their deaths occurred during the reign of Queen Mary Tudor), feeling that I too wanted to die as a martyr. It was in 1956. I asked Dr. N. B. Magruder, whom I mentioned earlier, did he not think that the highest level of devotion to Christ would be to die as a martyr. He smiled then wrote the aforementioned words on a piece of paper I carried with me for years: "My willingness to forsake any claim on God is the only evidence I have seen the divine glory." That statement sobered me. Agree or disagree, it suggested to me that my desire to be a martyr should be subordinate to my desire to honor the God of glory—however He wanted to use me.

My friend Josef Tson, whose words about total forgiveness changed my life forever, used to expect to die as a martyr. He suffered many years in Romania during the days of the Soviet Union. He wrote his doctoral thesis on martyrdom. He has since moved to America and lives in Portland, Oregon. He has become reconciled to the likelihood of not dying as a martyr.

My friend Arthur Blessitt, who is dying as I write these words, shared with me his disappointment that he would not die carrying his cross. It has been a major concession for him in his heart that he will die a natural death.

God will determine when and how each of us must die. I gave up the hope of dying as a martyr a long time ago, especially after Dr. Magruder's words to me. But who knows!

We spent three years living in Oxford (1973–1976). I walked by the old Balliol ditch, now Broad Street, day after day during those years. I used to stand by the spot—now a cross embedded into the pavement in Broad Street (next to Balliol College)—to commemorate the deaths of the Oxford martyrs. As I stood by that hallowed spot and gazed at the Sheldonian Theatre several hundred feet away, I prayed many times: "Lord, if I make it to the Sheldonian, please, please let me never ever forget this cross in the road." The Sheldonian is where the Oxford degrees are handed out. I knew if I outlived my respect and zeal for those men who died for Jesus in Oxford, I would be of no use to God.

As it happened, I made it to the Sheldonian in the spring of 1977. The twelve deacons of Westminster Chapel, who recommended me to be the minister of the chapel, accompanied by Dr. and Mrs. Martyn Lloyd-Jones, came to the ceremony.

One more personal story, very precious to me. Rev. Al

Dawson, our friend back in Fort Lauderdale, came to see Louise and me during our time in Oxford. I took him to the cross in the road in Broad Street. He secretly returned to that spot with his camera. Also an ingenious artist, Al presented me with an oil painting of his photo of Broad Street and the cross in the road—which shows both the cross and the Sheldonian Theatre. It hangs in our apartment in Nashville, where I have a conscious gaze at it every single day.

I have not forgotten the Oxford martyrs. Nor am I, I truly believe, afraid to die.

# PART III

## The Ugly—Satanic Fear

## CHAPTER 7

# Spiritual Warfare

We do not wrestle against flesh and blood, but
against the rulers, against the authorities, against the
cosmic powers over this present darkness, against
the spiritual forces of evil in the heavenly places.

—EPHESIANS 6:12

But the evil spirit answered them, "Jesus I know,
and Paul I recognize, but who are you?"

—ACTS 19:15

I want to be known in hell!

—ROLFE BARNARD (1904–1969)

WOULD YOU LIKE to be known in hell? I would. And
I will tell you why. It would mean that I am a
threat to the satanic world. I would love to be a threat
to the satanic world. I would far prefer to be famous in
hell than famous on earth, as I said in my book *Popular
in Heaven, Famous in Hell* (Charisma House). I would be
flattered to think that I really am a threat to the devil.
That would mean my ministry worries the devil, that I

am doing so much good for God that Satan is nervous about me, that I am threatening his interests. Of course, he knows about all of us who are Christians. But that does not mean all of us are necessarily a *threat* to him. I doubt that I am a threat to him, but I hope I might be before I go to heaven.

Satan is ugly. All that he does is ugly. One of his weapons is to make you afraid. Making people afraid is what he does. Spreading terror is his goal. God has not given us a spirit of fear (2 Tim. 1:7), but Satan will try to engender fear in you and me if he can.

You do not need to be afraid of the devil. A healthy respect? Yes. But do not be afraid of him. That is what he wants!

Satanic fear is the worst kind of fear there is. He wants you to be afraid of death. He wants you to be afraid of people. He wants you to be afraid of the future. He wants you to worry about the past. He wants you to take normal fears—being afraid of an approaching hurricane, caution when crossing a street, anxiety while awaiting the results of an examination, a plane falling, a virus—and exaggerate them. As I said, making people afraid is what he does.

One thing we should know about the devil up front: he is scared far, far more than you and I will ever be. He knows his end—punishment forever and ever in the lake of fire:

> And the devil who had deceived them was thrown
> into the lake of fire and sulfur where the beast

and the false prophet were, and they will be tormented day and night forever and ever.

—REVELATION 20:10

When Jesus began healing people and casting out demons, the evil spirits cried out, "What have you to do with us, O Son of God? Have you come here to torment us before the time?" (Matt. 8:29). We learn from this that the demons know who Jesus is—even if the world doesn't! The devil not only believes there is a God (Jas. 2:19) but that Jesus is the Son of God. We also learn from this that the devil knows his ultimate destiny in everlasting hell. Indeed, he is angry and full of fear and the desire for vengeance because "he knows that his time is short" (Rev. 12:12). What intensifies Satan's fear and anger is that we overcome "by the blood of the Lamb" (Rev. 12:11). This points yet again to the cross and the blood of Jesus—the constant, never-out-of-sight reminder that Satan was defeated by the death of Jesus Christ on the cross.

Because Satan is terrified, he wants to spread terror. The devil is afraid day and night—twenty-four hours a day, he wants you to be afraid. Misery loves company.

He also wants to make you feel guilty. He does not want you to have assurance of salvation. He is called the "accuser" (Rev. 12:10). He will magnify every fault or failure you have (we all have them) and try to convince you that God has not accepted you. As Jonathan Edwards once put it, Satan was trained in the heavenlies; he knows God's ways. His education surpassed learning in a university or seminary; he learned not from books but by beholding directly and firsthand the ways of the Most High God. Yes, the devil knows much of God's ways.

To put it in a crass, simple way: Imagine the top man in the CIA defecting to Russia's KGB. He would use his knowledge of the CIA to defeat the CIA. Possibly more than you and I can know them while we are on this earth, Satan before the revolt got to know much of God's ways but uses his knowledge for evil purposes. We cannot match his knowledge or power by ourselves; we must overcome by the "blood of the Lamb" and by our testimony (Rev. 12:11). This means that we are *vocal* in our praise and witness for the Lord Jesus Christ. The happy consequence of this is that we do not love our lives unto death. We know we are not our own; we are bought with the blood of Christ (1 Cor. 6:19–20). No wonder that we must honor the blood of Jesus!

Satan's chief enemy is Jesus Christ. Oh, how he hates the Son of God. No vocabulary in any language would come close to demonstrating how much Satan hates the Lord Jesus Christ. He hates any mention of the cross. He despises the blood that Jesus shed on the cross. After all, the cross—it cannot be stated too often—is what guaranteed his downfall. Until Easter morning the devil thought he had conquered the greatest victory of all time. He regarded himself as the architect of the crucifixion. He was sure he orchestrated all the events that led to Jesus' death: the chief priests' plan to kill Him (John 11:49–53), the betrayal by Judas Iscariot (John 13:2), the anger of

Herod toward Jesus (Luke 23:11), the unanimous request of the Jews to set Barabbas free and crucify Jesus (Matt. 27:20–23), the decision of Pontius Pilate to have Jesus crucified (Matt. 27:24–26), the Roman soldiers' glee in physically crucifying Jesus (Matt. 27:27–31), and the priests saying, "He saved others; he cannot save himself" (Matt. 27:42).

But on the day Jesus was raised from the dead Satan suddenly discovered that he not only failed; the crucifixion sealed his everlasting doom. This is described in the Book of Revelation. This, then, is why he hates the blood of Jesus. Had the "princes of this world" known what they were doing, "they would not have crucified the Lord of glory" (1 Cor. 2:8). The cross was the weapon of God to defeat Satan, sin, and death—the best kept secret since the creation of the world!

We don't know as much about the life of Jesus as we may like to know. Always remember this about the Bible regarding *any* subject: God has told us all we need to know—whether it be the hidden years of Jesus before His being baptized by John the Baptist, unfolding the whole meaning of all the parables, what all was going on in the earliest church that is barely explained in the Book of Acts, what was going on in the church after Peter and Paul died...I could go on and on. We all have questions that we would love to have the answers to.

As for the origin of the devil, we don't know as much as we would like to know. It is clear that there was a revolt in the heavenlies—sometime after creation but before the fall of man. We must avoid unprofitable speculation. But two New Testament passages must be taken into account.

What is absolutely clear is that all principalities and authorities were created by God:

> For by him all things were created, in heaven and on earth, visible and invisible, whether thrones or dominions or rules or authorities—all things were created through him and for him. And he is before all things, and in him all things hold together.
> —COLOSSIANS 1:16–17

At some stage the issue of the origin of evil emerges. I may say categorically that how and why evil emerged is unknowable. We can deduce some things that seem fairly clear. For one thing, there was a revolt in the heavenlies, probably before the creation of man. Satan is a creation of God (Col. 1:16–17). God did not create *fallen* angels. They, as all creation, were created without sin. Before the fall, Satan may have been called "Lucifer, son of the morning" (Isa. 14:12, KJV). Apparently, this was an angel of very high intelligence, although I am speculating. It is clear he was jealous of God. He apparently recruited every angel in the heavenlies to join in his revolt. How many? Who knows? Possibly a third of the angels, if that is what Revelation is referring to (Rev. 12:4). We don't know for sure, nor do we need to know. It is safe to assume, however, that all of the redeemed by the blood of Jesus have angels who guard them day and night (Heb. 1:14; Ps. 34:7).

I have been fascinated by the word *will* in Hebrews 1:14 (NIV): it suggests that an angel is dispatched to the people of God before they are converted, but who *will* be saved. Of course, God knows who will be saved; He knows the end from the beginning (Isa. 46:10). Many saved people testify how they sensed God being with them before they were converted—keeping them from danger, for example, or keeping them from sinning worse than they did. We may well see our angel in heaven. You can know this much about your angel: he resisted Satan's revolt, being well experienced in spiritual warfare.

Angels are utterly and totally devoted to God. They will not allow being worshipped. I have always been surprised that John, who should have known better, fell down to worship the angel who gave him the Book of Revelation (19:10; 22:8). However, it not only demonstrates John's willingness to show vulnerability but how secure he was in his relationship with God. In any case, this account means you and I should not talk to our angel—ever. This would be idolatry, one of the things Paul warned against (Col. 2:19). See also John's last word in his first epistle: "Little children, keep yourselves from idols" (1 John 5:21).

The angels that fell with Satan are not in everlasting hell yet; they are in *tartarus*, a Greek word sometimes translated "hell," as we will discuss. I wish translators had left *tartarus* untranslated so that it might take on its own meaning. See my book *Popular in Heaven, Famous in Hell* for more details about *tartarus*.

The revolt in heaven is shown in two places. The first appears to be the beginning of a sentence not completed by Peter. Why? You tell me! But it reads:

> If God did not spare angels when they sinned, but cast them into hell [Greek *tartarus*] and committed them to chains of gloomy darkness to be kept until the judgment.
>
> —2 PETER 2:4

The second is taken from a longer sentence in Jude:

> And the angels who did not stay within their own position of authority, but left their proper dwelling, he has kept in eternal chains under gloomy darkness until the judgment of the great day.
>
> —JUDE 6

But *tartarus* would seem to be a place where fallen angels—called demons—now reside. They exist to oppress and, when possible, possess human beings.

The evil spirit that talked back to the inexperienced man who was trying to cast out this demon was apparently in *tartarus*.

Can a true born-again Christian have a demon? Yes, in my opinion. I will return to this. This takes me back to two people I knew at the RAF Upper Heyford air base in Oxfordshire, England. While I was working on my research degree at Oxford, I was privileged to pastor a Southern Baptist church nearby. Two stories are worth sharing. First, we had a member who had many books on the occult, witchcraft, and demonology. I would not

140

regard him as being deeply spiritual. He was unfaithful in church attendance. He had very few books that were edifying, and the books (he had nearly a dozen) on the devil outnumbered them. He regarded this collection as evidence he was godly. This made me realize how the devil loves this kind of attention. He knew more about witchcraft than sound theology and loved stories about the occult.

Second, I met a Royal Air Force general who was a Christian. We talked about the possibility of demon possession. He argued that this is not possible today since Jesus' death defeated the powers of darkness. He was extremely naïve but would not be reasoned with. He not only thought it was impossible for a Christian to have a demon; he did not think a non-Christian could either. According to him, they don't exist at all—that is, since Jesus died on the cross.

This shows at least two things about the devil. Satan wants one of two things: a lot of attention or no attention at all. Regarding the latter, he would prefer that people not believe he exists. He would love to engender atheism, of course, but also unbelief in himself. Therefore remember: unbelief in the devil is the devil's work. If you don't believe in the existence of Satan, you show that the devil has already succeeded with you.

As for the devil loving lots of attention, I fear that some Christians do this. In two ways: (1) They are unnecessarily afraid of the devil. As I said earlier, we must have a healthy respect for the devil, but you don't need to be afraid of him—he would love that! (2) Some Christians, especially a lot of Charismatics, attribute anything that is not good (in their opinion) to the devil. Some of them not only see the devil on every bush, but they cannot believe that God would send COVID-19 as a judgment. Only the devil would do that, they say. Wrong. God takes the responsibility again and again for sending evil things. As for COVID, see my book *We've Never Been This Way Before* for my demonstrating that God is behind COVID-19—which I call His gracious judgment in order to get our attention. As Cardinal Timothy Dolan put it, "God is right in the middle of it," as quoted in that book.[1] By the way, we have not seen the end of what God is up to!

I can understand why many might not believe that a Christian can have a demon. They argue that the Holy Spirit cannot indwell an unclean vessel. That is logical. But, as James stated that both salt water and fresh water should not flow from a Christian—but they do— so a believer can sometimes stoop pretty low. "From the same mouth come blessing and cursing. My brothers, these things ought not to be so" (Jas. 3:10). True. But the fact is, said James, this is too often the case. A spark can cause a forest fire because the tongue is a "restless evil, full of deadly poison" (Jas. 3:8). Based on this, it seems plausible that James has set the stage for the possibility that a Christian could, at least sometimes, have a demon. Paul said we should walk by the Spirit and not "gratify the desires of the flesh." It shows that the desires of the flesh are present in the believer. "For the desires of the flesh are against the Spirit, and the desires of the Spirit are against the flesh, for these are opposed to each other to keep you from doing the things you want to do" (Gal. 5:16–17).

Neither James nor Paul is talking about a demon in a Christian. They are talking about the imperfection in Christians. We are not glorified yet. We will be (1 John 3:2; Rom. 8:30). But Christians can still be in the flesh. Paul refers to a fleshly Christian (1 Cor. 3:3); though immature, it shows that the flesh may sometimes be too plainly manifest. It is that which, I am of the opinion, might give the devil access. Not only that, but unforgiveness—willful bitterness—may be an invitation for the devil to make his way in (2 Cor. 2:13–14). I am not saying this is common, but it suggests the possibility. In any case it is a sobering warning that unforgiveness makes one vulnerable to the devil.

It is hard to show from the Bible that a Christian can be demon possessed. But let me relate three stories and then you can decide for yourself.

First, Dr. Martyn Lloyd-Jones told me this story. In a church where he preached annually in Wales, he noticed that friends of his were not in the service. He asked the host pastor where these friends were. As they were speaking the phone rang. It was Dr. Lloyd-Jones' friend, who said, "Oh doctor, I am sorry to miss you this year, but my wife is in bad shape, acting very strange, and I don't know what to do." The more they talked, the more the doctor was convinced what would be the next step forward.

He said to the pastor: "This is a clear case of demon possession. You must get one of your elders and go to their home and cast out the demon." The pastor replied, "Oh please, you do it." Dr. Lloyd-Jones replied, "Because I am a medical doctor, they will say there is a medical or psychological explanation. You and an elder can do it. As soon as you step into their house, pray for your own protection—to be covered by the blood of Christ— and start saying aloud, 'Jesus Christ is come in the flesh, Jesus Christ is come in the flesh, Jesus Christ is come in the flesh,' until you get a violent reaction, and then speak directly to the demon: 'Come out of her and go to the place of your appointment.'"

The pastor followed Dr. Lloyd-Jones' instructions and returned an hour later, amazed. "We did exactly what you said. The woman shrieked and fell out on the floor— and went limp when we commanded the demon to come out." Dr. Lloyd-Jones said the lady was back in church on the front row with her husband the next night, with a shine on her face.

Second, Hudson Taylor (1832–1905), a Brit and founder of the China Inland Mission, was a missionary to China. There was an occasion when he cast a demon out of a Chinese person. But the next day Hudson Taylor was paralyzed. He realized he forgot to pray for his own protection. He had other Christians gather around him, and they cast the demon out. Strange? Yes. But it is a fact in Hudson Taylor's life.

Third, a man named Anthony had been led to the Lord by one of our Pilot Lights when I was at Westminster Chapel. He showed up again to ask for prayer. He said he felt like razor blades were cutting inside his stomach. He looked pale and was in great pain. He added, shamefully, "I am sorry to tell you I attended a black mass." I then knew what to do, recalling the aforementioned story from Dr. Lloyd-Jones. I started saying, "Jesus Christ is come in the flesh, Jesus Christ is come in the flesh, Jesus Christ is come in the flesh." His face became twisted, and he looked afraid. I then said, "In the name of Jesus come out of him and go to the place of your appointment." As I spoke his face looked gnarled and his voice filled with fear. Then he went limp. I had him sit inside Westminster Chapel. In a few minutes he came out. His face had color. He smiled and said, "I don't know what you did, but I feel so good."

It has been observed by some that a difference between people being saved in Latin America and the United States is this: in Latin America and South America they cast demons out at the time of a person's profession of faith. In America they are sent on their way, sometimes with little or no follow-up.

When Paul says, "We do not wrestle against flesh and blood" but against "the authorities" and "spiritual forces" in the heavenlies (Eph. 6:12), two questions can be asked. First, does Paul speak for all Christians? In other words, can you and I assume that we too automatically have this battle because we are saved? Or is this something Paul came into and shares with us? I am inclined to think that not all Christians know about this. Some discover it, some don't.

The second question: Does Paul mean that he does not regard people—"flesh and blood"—as the enemy but rather the devil? In other words, has he learned not to take opposition personally but instead sees the devil being behind it? If so, it suggests that you and I should not see a person who opposes us or doesn't like us as being the origin of opposition but that he or she is being coerced by Satan. This would be why Jesus said to Peter, "Get behind me, Satan!" (Matt. 16:23). He did not accuse Peter of not being saved. He did not get angry with Peter himself. He saw that Peter was saying something that Satan originated.

Whether or not you and I experience what Paul relates, this much is true: the possibility exists. It is there all the time. Perhaps you can avoid it by staying away from a closer walk with God! But as surely as you walk in the light (1 John 1:7) and please God fully, you will disturb God's enemy for sure.

As Jonathan Edwards put it, when the church is revived, so is the devil. And when you and I are revived, so do we get more acquainted with Christ's chief enemy. It means we are doing something right. It also suggests that we will be known in hell—that is, *tartarus.*

## CHAPTER 8

# The Evil Day

Finally, be strong in the Lord and in the strength of his might. Put on the whole armor of God, that you may be able to stand against the schemes of the devil. For we do not wrestle against flesh and blood, but against the rulers, against the authorities, against the cosmic powers over this present darkness, against the spiritual forces of evil in heavenly places. Therefore take up the whole armor of God, that you may be able to withstand in the evil day, and having done all, to stand firm. Stand therefore, having fastened on the belt of truth, and having put on the breastplate of righteousness, and, as shoes for your feet, having put on the readiness given by the gospel of peace. In all circumstances take up the shield of faith, with which you can extinguish all the flaming darts of the evil one; and take the helmet of salvation, and the sword of the Spirit, which is the word of God, praying at all times in the Spirit, with all prayer and supplication.

—EPHESIANS 6:10–18

The worst thing that can happen to a man
is to succeed before he is ready.
—DR. MARTYN LLOYD-JONES

I RAN INTO A friend at Spring Harvest (a popular Easter festival in Britain) some years ago and asked, "What are you doing these days?" He replied: "I'm into spiritual warfare." My heart sank. I knew he would not last long in it, that as a specialized ministry it was a fad that some Charismatics were running to. I can't imagine anyone voluntarily entering into a ministry like that. Whereas you don't need to be afraid of the devil, you don't want to pick a fight with him either. Forgive me if this sounds strong, but no one in his or her right mind should challenge Satan to a duel.

When Ellie Mumford was used of God to bring the Toronto Blessing to London's Holy Trinity Brompton in 1994, she made the passing observation that, during her time in Toronto, she never heard "spiritual warfare" mentioned once. She seemed to see this as a positive thing. I know that is the way I interpreted it. But many Charismatics had been enthralled with this emphasis, and it was getting them nowhere spiritually.

If you attack the devil, you are out of your depth. You will lose every time. You are no match for Satan when you think you can enter his territory and put him in his place. The only time you are a match for the devil is *when he attacks you* and you are ready for him.

Spiritual warfare must be *defensive* if you expect to win. Notice the classic passage on spiritual warfare cited earlier—Ephesians 6:12–18—and observe that the word *stand* is put there by Paul four times in four verses. And the whole context is based upon how to cope when the devil *attacks.* You have a glorious promise of coping without being defeated when he attacks you. But you have no promise like that if you launch out into the deep over your head, going into gloomy spiritual places without him attacking you first. If you attack him, you are on your own. When he attacks you, you have the promises of God on how to cope.

It is like the matter of trial, or testing. James said to count it pure joy when you fall into various kinds of trial (Jas. 1:2). Since "pure joy" and "trial" can come together, someone might say, "I need some joy, therefore I will look for a trial." Don't be a fool! The trial will come soon enough. Don't go out looking for a trial.

This is why Jesus gave the petition in the Lord's Prayer, "Lead us not into temptation" (Matt. 6:13). We must pray for God's guidance daily. Louise and I pray the Lord's Prayer together daily. As we should not go out looking for a trial, so also we should pray, "Lord, may it please You that I am not led today *into* temptation." The Greek word *peirasmos* means "testing," "trial," or "temptation." Any of these words would have been a valid translation for the Lord's Prayer.

Dr. Michael Eaton has made the helpful suggestion that we might emphasize the word *into.* We should pray that God will graciously spare us of being thrown into the deep end. Pray therefore to avoid trial. Pray to avoid testing. Pray to avoid temptation. Pray therefore that God will be pleased to lead us in a trouble-free direction. But if after that we *do* fall into trial, James has a word for us: count it all joy! When it happened to you but you did not cause it, you qualify for great joy! The word *count* is essentially the same Greek word (*egesasthe*) as *impute* or *imputed*, which is used three times in Romans 4:3–5.

As God imputes righteousness to us by our faith, so you and I should impute joy to a trial. God counts us righteousness when we may be ungodly; we count a trial pure joy although we may *feel* no joy at first. This means that if you are found in a trial—one you *fell* into but did not bring on yourself—you qualify to impute *joy* to that trial! This is because if you *dignify the trial*, you will come out of it smelling like a rose. You will find yourself upgraded to a higher level of God's grace and favor. What is more, you will thank God for the very trial you initially were tempted to complain about. I can personally testify that the greatest trial Louise and I ever faced in our lives, we now thank God for. Indeed, it was the best thing that ever happened to us. This is why we should impute joy *by faith* to a trial in advance of how we feel.

Every trial is a test from God, an examination. Either you pass or fail. He keeps score. If you fail—as I did again and again and again for too many years—God says, "Sorry about this, but I will have to arrange another trial for you." The good news is, God gives second chances. The bad news is, if we don't start dignifying trials instead of moaning, groaning, grumbling, murmuring, and complaining, we have to keep resitting trials. Not that they are all the same, but all are tests to see whether you will—at last—start dignifying the trial instead of grumbling.

Why count it pure joy? It is because the happy outcome of dignifying a trial is so sweet. The trial is a prerequisite to such joy.

At the same time we are not to go looking for a trial. We pray to avoid it as long as we can, but when the "evil day" comes, James would tell us to take it with both hands and show how much we really do believe God to be in control!

The evil day. Yes. That is what Paul calls it. It is when God gives Satan permission to have a go at you. He did it with Job. He will do it with you and me.

Trial, then, is what leads to great growth:

> We rejoice in our sufferings, knowing that suffering produces endurance, and endurance produces character, and character produces hope, and hope does not put us to shame.
>
> —ROMANS 5:3–5

Paul uses the expression "the evil day" in Ephesians 6:13. David in the Psalms refers to "the day of my trouble" (Ps. 86:7). "He will hide me in his shelter in the day of trouble" (Ps. 27:5). God says, "Call on me in the day of trouble" (Ps. 50:15). The question is: Is Satan the architect of a "day of trouble"? Is this what Paul means by the "evil day"? The answer, I believe, is two things: First, there are days that are difficult, when things go wrong. If we begin to complain as soon as things are not smooth, the devil will jump in and magnify what otherwise would have passed over fairly quickly. I do think there are days in which, by God's permission and sovereign design, Satan is given an opportunity to attack us.

One of the greatest sermons I ever heard was by Josef Tson at Westminster Chapel. He called his sermon "Mysterious Reasons for Suffering." One of the reasons Josef offered was that the angels wanted to see if Job—who had everything but lost everything—would curse God under extremely difficult circumstances. Likewise, the angels are watching us to see how we will react in an evil day. The Book of Job is one long explanation of what could be called the evil day. But God started it (Job 1:8). God ended it (Job 38:1). Job tells us in the end what he learned: "Now I know that you can do all things, and that no purpose of yours can be thwarted" (Job 42:2).

In other words, there are days that we ourselves can make evil—by our grumbling. But they could be short-lived if we would consider the trial "pure joy." However, there are special days—of severe trial—such as with Job that last a while. But this too will work together for good (Rom. 8:28).

One of the most memorable days of my life was when Billy Graham came to Westminster Chapel to spend time with me just before preaching for us two days later. He volunteered this information: "Before every crusade we have ever had there has been an attack of the devil on us. Sometimes it will be members of the team falling out with each other. But something will happen every time." He himself had been struck with an odd illness just before he came to see me. He went to the hospital straight from our time together and almost needed to cancel his preaching engagement with us. He came to us on the Sunday night with a nosebleed. A box of tissues sat on the pulpit as he spoke.

In a word: there are two kinds of evil days: (1) when we make them such by our lack of faith, and (2) when Satan initiates an attack.

Moreover, Paul tells us how to cope in Ephesians 6:10: "Be strong in the Lord and in the strength of his might." If we do this, we will be able to resist the devil.

It is often said that the best defense is a good offense. But not with the devil! This would be true in football. Basketball. Soccer. But not in a fight with Satan. Let him start it. If we are strong in the Lord, we will be able to withstand the evil day and show, once again, that Satan *always overreaches himself.*

## WHAT DOES IT MEAN TO STAND?

As we saw earlier, Paul uses the word *stand* four times. What do we do when the devil attacks? We *stand.* This means:

1. We don't walk.

2. We don't run.

3. We don't trip.

4. We don't go backwards.

5. We don't fall.

What is required of you and me when Satan attacks is one thing: stand. Until the storm passes by, our weapon is to stand. How do we make spiritual progress in a severe trial? Stand. Wait. The storm will pass. All trials have a time scale. We may think, "This will never end." But it will. And when it's over, it's over. In heaven you get a report card—pass or fail. If you pass, congratulations! This means you are growing.

How will you know if you pass the test? You will sense God's smile by the internal testimony of the Holy Spirit. If you dignified the trial, you will know it. If you complained the whole time, you will feel it—a sadness, a sense of God's displeasure, will settle on you. It means that God will come back in the future with another trial! The good news: He stays with us until we pass. I am ashamed to admit it, but I was a Christian for many years before I finally woke up and began to dignify the trial. God is gracious and patient.

However, there is one salient sentence in Ephesians 6:12 you must not overlook. This passage is introduced by these words, "Be strong in the Lord and in the strength of his might." In other words, *what prepares you for the satanic attack?* It is being strong in the Lord and in the strength of His mighty power. This means preparation nonstop, twenty-four hours a day, seven days a week. You never know when the devil will attack.

Peter said,

> Be sober-minded; be watchful. Your adversary the
> devil prowls around like a roaring lion, seeking
> someone to devour. Resist him, firm in your faith,
> knowing that the same kinds of suffering are being
> experienced by your brotherhood throughout the
> world.
>
> —1 PETER 5:8–9

James said virtually the same thing:

> Submit yourselves therefore to God. Resist the
> devil, and he will flee from you.
>
> —JAMES 4:7

Note James' order: (1) Submitting yourselves therefore
to God. This is the same thing as being "strong in the
Lord," then (2) resisting the devil. If you and I have not
made ample preparation by being strong in the Lord,
Satan almost certainly will not be seen to have overreached himself.

That said, our enemy the devil is a conquered foe. He
lost at the cross. Resist him. This is done by *standing*!

Never underestimate the importance of preparation.
This means being ready. Staying ready. You never know
when Satan will attack—much like the second coming!
We know neither the day nor the hour Jesus will come.
Jesus told us to be ready (Matt. 24:45–51). Likewise,
agree James and Peter, be sober minded, be ready. Be
ready for the attack.

If you *stand*, having been prepared by being strong in

the Lord, you will find that the devil overreaches himself as he did when he thought the crucifixion of Jesus was his idea. As I said, had the authorities and powers known what was going on, they would not have crucified the Lord of glory (1 Cor. 2:8).

One should covet the best—or "higher"—gifts of the Spirit (1 Cor. 12:31). One of the most important gifts is the distinguishing between spirits (1 Cor. 12:9). The first thing we should know about this gift is having the discernment to recognize the genuine Holy Spirit. In my book *Pigeon Religion*, I attempt to make the case that some people hastily assume that God is being manifested when it is really pigeon religion! Pigeons and doves are in the same family. Anatomically, pigeons and doves are exactly the same. But temperamentally they are different. You can train a pigeon, but you cannot train a dove. A pigeon is boisterous; a dove is gentle. A genuine gift of being able to distinguish between spirits is important, especially in this book.

Whereas Peter said that the devil can come as a roaring lion, Paul said he can come as an angel of light (2 Cor. 11:14). It is true that the devil may be prominent in places that do witchcraft and in places of prostitution, but he may also possess the most sophisticated and dignified people. He may be a banker, a physician, an accountant, or a politician. What Paul is saying in 2 Corinthians 11:14 is that nothing should surprise us.

As I keep saying, Satan thought he was the architect of the crucifixion of Jesus. But he was defeated by the power of the cross and the resurrection of Jesus. Jesus was "delivered up according to the definite plan and foreknowledge of God" (Acts 2:23). God outwitted Satan by His predetermined plan, the blood Jesus shed and the resurrection. Indeed, as the disciples prayed—which shows their theology—

> For truly in this city there were gathered together against your holy servant Jesus, whom you anointed, both Herod and Pontius Pilate, along with the Gentiles and the peoples of Israel, to do whatever your hand and your plan had predestined to take place.
>
> —ACTS 4:27–28

Satan overreached himself. He always does. But if we don't "stand" when the evil day comes, he may appear to win. This is why we overcome Satan by the blood of the Lamb and the word of our testimony (Rev. 12:11). We must testify—be vocal and unafraid to take the stand that is necessary.

## THE IMPORTANCE OF HAVING A SOUND THEOLOGY

I was in Bimini a few years ago to do some bonefishing while on vacation. This was when we were still located at Westminster Chapel. I turned on the television one evening and watched a young evangelist speak. It was the first time I saw him. I had not heard of him (being in England tended to keep me out of touch with what was going on in America). I had a negative feeling. Though gifted, he seemed so shallow theologically. A couple of years later, lo and behold, this same preacher was in London and introduced himself to me. I also heard that he was going to have meetings in a major American city—that he was going to attack the devil and the evils of this city. When I heard that I cringed. The result of his attack was that he not only failed but his ministry was permanently sidelined.

Because we had met, I wrote him a letter and quoted Dr. Lloyd-Jones: "The worst thing that can happen to a man is to succeed before he is ready."[1] I urged him to be in no hurry to get back into prominence. He who humbles himself will be exalted; he who exalts himself shall be abased (Luke 14:11). Pride goes before a downfall (Prov. 16:18). I felt that if he were to humble himself and wait on God's timing, he might still have a future. His failure was, in my opinion, a textbook evidence of Dr. Lloyd-Jones' caution. As far as I could tell, although he thanked me for my letter, he totally ignored my advice. He is now yesterday's man when he might have been today's and tomorrow's man.

When I initially saw him on TV while in Bimini, my feeling was that he was not ready for the success he seemed to have—not necessarily because of his age but because of the lack of a sound understanding of the Bible. I learned later that, sadly, prominent people were pushing him and praising him. The eventual proof of his not being ready for success was his lack of knowledge.

This was further evidenced by his naïve notion that he could attack the devil and beat him.

"My people are destroyed for lack of knowledge" (Hos. 4:6). God wants His people to know at least two things: knowledge of His Word and knowledge of His ways. The saddest thing nowadays among too many Christians—and church leaders—is their lack of reading and knowing their Bibles. This includes pastors. I urge you, dear reader, not only to have a Bible reading plan that takes you through the Bible in a year but a prayer life that shows how much you want to know the Lord. We get to know anybody by spending time with them. So too with God. Spend much time in prayer and reading God's Word. "My people have not known my ways," God lamented when referring to the children of Israel (Heb. 3:10). I used to urge all the members of Westminster Chapel to spend thirty minutes a day in prayer and reading the Bible. One of my deacons, now in heaven, spent one hour a day praying for me for nearly twenty-five years. I urge ministers to pray at least an hour a day. Martin Luther spent two hours a day in prayer. John Wesley spent two hours a day in prayer. But where are the Luthers and Wesleys of this world today?

I'm sorry, but the average church leader—according to a very reliable poll—spends four minutes a day in quiet time.

The early church had a robust view of the sovereignty of God. It is utterly lacking in the church today, speaking generally. All attempts to do "spiritual warfare" that

I have seen personally have emanated from a shallow understanding of God's power and sovereignty.

Spiritual warfare will be successful when we are equipped and ready for the devil's attack. I must repeat: don't attack the devil. No one is a match for him. But if he attacks and you are spiritually ready, he will be seen to have overreached himself—as happened on Good Friday and Easter.

CHAPTER 9

# Collective Evil

If the foundations are destroyed, what
can the righteous do?

—PSALM 11:3

The greatest evils in the world will not be carried out by men with guns, but by men
with suits sitting behind desks.

—C. S. LEWIS (1898–1963)

I VISITED THE AUSCHWITZ concentration camp almost fifty years ago. When I saw that tall and wide smokestack just inside the gate next to a railroad track, I wondered if it was what I thought it was. It was. It was situated in the gas chambers that cremated Jewish people in 1944. I am not saying I was traumatized. But maybe I was. I can only say that to this day whenever I see a smokestack—whether in a factory or a crematorium—I think of Auschwitz. It left me with a horrible feeling that is revived whenever I see a smokestack.

It is hard to imagine that a human being—of ancient times or modern times—could do such evil as organized by Adolf Hitler (1889–1945), leading to the deaths of six million Jews. He was the evil architectural mind that gave birth to the idea of getting rid of all Jews and having them shipped to places like Auschwitz for their extermination and cremation. I have read stories about him, and also Adolf Eichmann (1906–1962), who carried out the wicked scheme. Reports say he personally watched the Jews' suffering with glee.

How could a person conceive of such evil and carry it out? One thinks of the alleged evil acts of the Roman emperor Nero (37 BC–AD 68). Or the deeds of Josif Stalin (1878–1953). He executed millions; millions also starved to death at his direction. We have seen how ISIS people enjoy beheading innocent people, sawing their heads off before TV cameras. I will spare the reader of listing more heinous activities and wickedness.

Here is the question: How can a person be so wicked, so evil, so horrible, so terrible?

If, however, we are to listen to theologian Reinhold Niebuhr (1892–1971), evil is not to be traced back to the individual but to the collective behavior of humanity. He wrote a book called *Moral Man and Immoral Society*. He argues that people are more likely to sin as members of groups than as individuals. It is a most naïve view of human nature. Niebuhr was part of the popular neo-orthodoxy movement of the mid-twentieth century. By taking this view Niebuhr rejected not only the classic Christian teaching of the full inspiration of Holy

Scripture generally but the doctrine of original sin particularly as taught by St. Augustine (354–430).

Niebuhr's era paralleled a rising, ever-increasing, and widespread notion that man is basically good. People are essentially good, many want to say. You simply need to look for the good in people, and you will find it. As I was writing this chapter I saw a TV commercial that said, "Love is in you, pass it on." This kind of thinking coheres with the idea that man is certainly not evil but is essentially good. You might therefore say, "But you do see good things people do for humanity all the time, is this not true?" Of course it is. Jesus implied this in the famous parable of the Good Samaritan (Luke 10:29–37). It is an example of the doctrine of "common grace," to be examined below.

Niebuhr, greatly admired by President Jimmy Carter, was awarded the Presidential Medal of Freedom in 1964 when Lyndon Johnson was president. This is a typical example of the theological liberalism plus racism, legalized abortion, and the acceptance of same-sex marriage that has, in my opinion, brought the judgment of God on America, as I show in my book *We've Never Been This Way Before.*

St. Augustine suggested the four stages of man:

- Man was created *able to sin.*

- After the fall man was *not able not to sin.*

- After regeneration man was *able not to sin.*

- At glorification in heaven man will be *not able to sin.*

The traditional teaching of the natural depravity of man has been overthrown by the church generally in our generation. This teaching, however, does not suggest that all people are as bad as they could be. But the *potential* for evil resides in every person from the moment of their birth. It is by grace that people are not as bad as they could be. The teaching of man's natural depravity does not take into account the Protestant teaching of God's common grace—"special grace in nature," as one Protestant reformer put it. Augustine's teaching shows that all people are sinners, just as the Bible teaches:

> What then? Are we Jews any better off? No, not at all. For we have already charged that all, both Jews and Greeks, are under sin, as it is written: "None is righteous, no not one; no one understands; no one seeks for God. All have turned aside; together they have become worthless; no one does good, not even one. Their throat is an open grave; they use their tongues to deceive. The venom of asps is under their lips. Their mouth is full of curses and bitterness. Their feet are swift to shed blood; in their paths are ruin and misery, and the way of peace they have not known. There is no fear of God before their eyes." Now we know that whatever the law says it speaks to those who are under the law, so that every mouth may be stopped, and the whole world may be held accountable to God. For by works of the law no human being will be justified in his sight, since through the law comes knowledge of sin. But now the righteousness of God has been manifested apart from the law,

> although the law and the prophets bear witness to
> it—the righteousness through faith in Jesus Christ
> for all who believe. For there is no distinction: for
> all have sinned and fall short of the glory of God.
> —ROMANS 3:9–23

The view that man is a sinner and in need of a Savior is the foundation of the gospel, as taught by Paul.

What Paul says in these verses in Romans shows the state of humankind *after the fall*—that is, the way all people are born. We are born "dead" (Eph. 2:1). This means that man is unable not to sin unless the Spirit of God imparts life.

What Paul writes in Romans 3 describes the state into which you and I were born. In sin we were conceived (Ps. 51:5). We go astray from birth "speaking lies." You do not have to teach a child how to lie!

To put it another way, "all have sinned and fall short of the glory of God" (Rom. 3:23). There is no difference at this point between a Jew and a Gentile. A Roman or a German. An American or a Spaniard. Romans 3 describes the condition into which Nero was born. It may take a Hitler or a Stalin to convince the world of the potential danger of sin, but the Holy Spirit can fall on the saintliest person on earth and lead them to cry out, "Woe is me!" (Isa. 6:5). Sin is the natural condition into which Hitler was born. Stalin. Billy Graham. You and me.

It is therefore only the Holy Spirit that will truly enable one to see clearly one's own sin—or even to appreciate what sin is generally. One does not need to be a Hitler or a Stalin to be a sinner. Pride and unbelief—both chief examples of sin—are at the root of evil. Unless the Holy Spirit Himself moves in us we will *never* see pride and unbelief as serious maladies. Most people would say that pride is harmless, even a good thing; it motivates one to accomplish things, as we saw when dealing with Ecclesiastes 4:4.

The question is, what turns a person—who is born into sin like the rest of humankind—into a monster to be a Nero or a Hitler? I answer: demon possession. We are told that Satan entered Judas Iscariot. How else could anybody be so evil, having beheld the miracles of Jesus, His sermons, His parables, His love for sinners, His dialogues with the Pharisees and Sadducees, not to mention being taught how to pray? It is not normal human depravity that does such a wicked deed. Judas needed outside help—help from the devil himself. Here are three scriptures worth noting:

> The devil had already put it in the heart of Judas Iscariot, Simon's son, to betray him.
> —JOHN 13:2

> Then after he had taken the morsel of bread, Satan entered into him.
> —JOHN 13:27

> Then Satan entered into Judas called Iscariot, who was of the number of the twelve.
> —LUKE 22:3

My explanation then for the Neros and Stalins of this world is summed up in one word: the demonic. It is when Satan—or one of his fallen angels—enters into the body and mind of a human being. Sometimes it is more than one demon. Mary Magdalene had seven demons before she was delivered (Mark 16:9; Luke 8:2). In Mark's account of the Gerasene demoniac, Jesus asked for his name. He replied, "My name is Legion, for we are many" (Mark 5:9). When Jesus healed a man with an unclean spirit, he cried out, "What have you to do with us, Jesus of Nazareth? Have you come to destroy us? I know who you are—the Holy One of God" (Mark 1:24). Note the word *us* in Mark 1:24, implying there was more than one demon in this person. So too in Matthew's account: "Have you come here to torment us before the time?" (Matt. 8:29).

Note two things from the previous paragraphs. First, it shows that the devil knows his destiny. He is depicted in the Book of Revelation as being full of anger because he knows that "his time is short" (Rev. 12:12). Second, it shows how the devil believes in God! This is what James says: "Even the demons believe—and shudder" (Jas. 2:19). Belief here does not mean truth but rather belief in God's existence. Not only that, but the devil has an orthodox view of God: that God is one (Jas. 2:19) and that Jesus is the Holy One of God (Mark 1:24).

A woman had a "disabling spirit for eighteen years. She was bent over and could not fully straighten herself." Jesus said to her, "You are free from your disability"

(Luke 13:11–12). Does this mean that the "disabling spirit" was demonic? Possibly. Was the woman with the discharge of blood for twelve years (one Christian medic said it referred to a woman who never stopped having her periods) demon-possessed? I don't know.

There are questions about the demonic that I cannot explain. For example, how could a child be demon-possessed from childhood? I don't know. But major television networks have given reports of children with demons. One report said that in one state children walked up walls, levitated, and spoke in strange voices.

I am no expert in this area, nor do I care to be. I prefer to let some things remain a mystery. When Moses wanted to understand how a bush could be on fire and not be consumed, God told him to take off his shoes and worship (Exod. 3:5–6). There are some things that God does not want us to understand. We must take off our shoes.

I will, however, relate two stories. During my final two years at Westminster Chapel, we had weekly healing services following the preaching. One Sunday evening a lady from Peru came to me and said, "Heal my husband." I said, "Whatever do you mean, 'heal your husband'?" She replied, "Last Sunday you prayed for me. I had snake bite years ago. My right leg was swollen—big. The next morning it was normal, as the other. No doctor, no medicine. Now heal my husband." She had a lot of faith! More than I had. But I said to her husband, "What is your problem?" He said: "I don't sleep. I have not had a good night's sleep in twenty-five years. The spirits kick me out of bed." A deacon joined me, and we anointed him with oil. We made no attempt to cast out a demon, although that was obviously his problem. He returned the following week to say, "I slept three nights this week, first time in twenty-five years. Would you have another go?" We did. The following week he reported, "I slept seven nights. Like a baby." They remained with us until I retired. The problem never returned.

Should I have cast out the demon? I am sure some might have done this. We simply prayed as we always did, anointing with oil according to James 5:14. Demon possession may be the cause of sickness. I am uneasy with positing that the demonic is behind all illnesses.

All that being said, I return to Reinhold Niebuhr's view that sin is not to be traced to an individual but to the evil that comes from collective society. As I stated earlier, this is a naïve view of man and sin—and contrary to Holy Scripture. However, I do accept that collective society can magnify evil and be responsible for unthinkable atrocities. Auschwitz can be explained not only by Hitler but by a widespread view—Nazism—that spread hatred for Jews. It was based on racial superiority. It is the same thing as White supremacy, a view consciously and unconsciously held by too many Americans. God hates it. Just because some people don't *feel* God's hatred for racism does not mean God does not feel it. Indeed, in the same way that Christians can say, "God bless you," instead of giving people food and shelter—and feel not the slightest sense of sinfulness for their avoiding responsibility—so many of us White Christians don't want to contemplate the hurt that many African Americans feel.

In the same way that many White Americans—including born-again Christians—feel no shame for not feeling what African Americans feel, so do we participate in the racism that has hurt Black Americans and grieved the heart of God.

It is true that individuals can be racists. Of course. And that not all White Americans are racists. Thank God. But the collective sin of racism by millions of White people—including Evangelicals—has been, in my opinion, equal to how Nazism led to Auschwitz.

Yes. Far more than six million Jews being exterminated in Auschwitz during World War II is also the fact that Black Americans have been marginalized, hurt, hated, and neglected by racism.

Racism is a collective evil.

There is no end to how collective evil has brought fear to this world. To call it "ugly" seems so weak to describe what collective evil can be. As C. S. Lewis put it, the greatest evils are not from guns but from men in suits behind desks. From political parties (both Democrat and Republican) and the media (both CNN and Fox News) to the banking and educational systems (from grade schools to universities); from the entertainment world (both Hollywood and the television networks) to the issues regarding the environment; from foreign policy to the church generally.

There will come a day in which God will clear His name. Almighty God is the most maligned person in the universe. The problem of evil is universally and categorically laid at God's feet. We blame Him for everything.

One difference between a Christian and a non-Christian is this: Christians clear God's name *now*; one day every knee shall bow and every tongue confess that Jesus Christ is Lord to the glory of God the Father (Phil. 2:8–11)—and then affirm the holiness, justice, and love of God.

Perhaps the greatest sense of satanic fear is the fallout from COVID-19. Satan has exploited and capitalized on COVID, which in my opinion is God's gracious judgment. For those who do not have a robust conviction regarding the sovereignty of God, the fear that has been caused by COVID is enormous.

There are those who say that only the devil would bring COVID since God only does nice, positive things. Really?

> I form light and create darkness, I make well-being and create calamity. I am the LORD who does all these things. Shower, O heavens, from above, and let the clouds rain down righteousness; let the earth open, that salvation and righteousness may bear fruit; let the earth cause them both to sprout; I the LORD have created it.
>
> —ISAIAH 45:7–8

> See, I am setting before you today a blessing and a curse: the blessing if you obey the commandments

of the LORD your God, which I command you today, and the curse, if you do not obey the commandments of the LORD your God.
—DEUTERONOMY 11:26–28

Could the God of the Bible even cause fear? "Surely not," say some people. But here is what Moses said:

The LORD will give you there a trembling heart and failing eyes and a languishing soul. Your life shall hang in doubt before you. Night and day you shall be in dread and have no assurance of your life. In the morning you shall say, "If only it were evening!" and at evening you shall say, "If only it were morning!" because of the dread that your heart shall feel, and the sights that your eyes shall see.
—DEUTERONOMY 28:65–67

Although these warnings in Deuteronomy refer to ancient Israel, they came from God Almighty, the Father of our Lord Jesus Christ. Not only that, but countless thousands since COVID have experienced fear not unlike that description. One of the most obvious fallouts from COVID is fear. As I said, it is my view that God is behind COVID. Or, to quote Cardinal Timothy Dolan, archbishop of New York, when asked, "Where is God in COVID?" he answered, "He's right in the middle of it."

Some who deny the inspiration of Holy Scripture want to say that the God of the Old Testament is different from the God of the New Testament. Not true at all. First of all, Jesus never apologized for the God of the Old Testament. That is His Father!

God is in control. Supreme control. Our Lord Jesus Christ controls the universe by His power (Heb. 1:3). The same God who gave Satan permission to test Job is the Lord God who still is in charge of whatever the devil does. What is more, to those who refuse to curse God, as Job refused to do, will be the precious experience to say, "I know that you can do all things, and that no purpose of yours can be thwarted" (Job 42:2).

I challenge you to see what God will do for those who dignify every trial God allows.

## CHAPTER 10

# The Way Forward

Indeed, what I have forgiven, if I have forgiven anything, has been for your sake in the presence of Christ,
so that we would not be outwitted by Satan; for we
are not ignorant of his designs [not ignorant of his
devices—KJV; not unaware of his schemes—NIV].

—2 CORINTHIANS 2:10–11

Every time you forgive you disappoint the devil.

—RICK WARREN

THE BEST WEAPON in spiritual warfare is total forgiveness. If bitterness, unforgiveness, and holding
grudges is in our hearts, we will inevitably fail when the
evil day comes. You will lose every time; Satan will win
every time.

There is no human condition that puts Satan on the
fast track toward our defeat like unforgiveness.

I fear there are those who enter the area of spiritual
warfare—passing by the need for total forgiveness—with
the assumption that they can talk plainly and directly
to the devil, as if one says to Satan, "Get lost, devil, in

Jesus' name." I have observed people who are out of their depth but who want to address the devil like that. They assume a high level of spirituality and authority. Some of these people don't know their Bibles but want to demonstrate what they can do. "A little learning is a dangerous thing," as Alexander Pope (1688–1744) put it.

Even if you have the gift of miracles (1 Cor. 12:10) but use this gift while living in bitterness, you will pay a dear price down the road. King Saul's gift flourished, yes, when he was not right with God (1 Sam. 19:23–24), but the day came all too soon that he said, "I have played the fool" (1 Sam. 26:21, KJV).

When you gauge the proportion of space the New Testament gives to spiritual warfare and compare it to the place it holds with some Christians and church leaders, you will find that the latter often give far, far more attention to it than the New Testament does. Indeed, too many Christians today give the devil more attention and show more fear of the devil than they do the fear of God.

I have in other books made the observation that there is a silent divorce in the church, speaking generally, between the Word and the Spirit. In a divorce some children stay with the mother, some with the father. In this divorce there are those on the "Word" side and those on the "Spirit" side. I have also noted that Word people emphasize the "fruits" of the Spirit (Gal. 5:22); Spirit people tend to emphasize the "gifts" (1 Cor. 12:8–10).

The practice of total forgiveness should be welcomed

and embraced by both sides. It is the greatest need in the church today—whether you are on the Word side or the Spirit side. Not only that, but total forgiveness is the *hardest* thing to do under the sun. It takes minimal discipline to enter into spiritual warfare. It takes a *lot* of discipline to forgive totally those who have maligned you, hurt you, lied about you, and wanted to destroy you. It is easier to forget total forgiveness and plunge into casting out devils.

Paul's classic statement on spiritual warfare in Ephesians 6:10–18 shows the need for personal discipline in one's own life. This is why Paul begins with the words, "Be strong in the Lord" (Eph. 6:10). He does not merely say, "Be strong." He says, "Be *strong in the Lord*" (emphasis added). This assumes a relationship with Jesus that enables you to be equipped when the evil day comes. And it will come.

Whereas Paul uses the phrase "in Christ" again and again and again in Ephesians—meaning our justification and security—he uses it differently in Ephesians 6:10. He is talking about a personal intimacy with the Lord Jesus Christ. It means *knowing* Him through the power of His resurrection and suffering (Phil. 3:10).

The teaching of forgiveness is the most neglected aspect in the church, not least when it comes to dealing with the devil.

We are no match for the devil if there is the slightest bitterness in our hearts. As soon as Paul said that we should not grieve the Holy Spirit of God, he added: "Let all bitterness and wrath and anger" be put away from you, then concluded: "Forgiving one another, as God in Christ forgave you" (Eph. 4:30–32). Bitterness and unforgiveness is not the only way we can grieve the Holy Spirit, but it is the chief way we grieve Him. That is why Paul mentions this first after his admonition that we do not grieve the Spirit.

Bitterness opens the door of our hearts to Satan. I am not saying the devil possesses those who struggle to forgive. We all struggle in this area. But Paul made it astonishingly clear that the devil can easily outwit us if we do not forgive (2 Cor. 2:11). God will not bend the rule for any of us.

Whereas the gifts are "without repentance" (Rom. 11:29, KJV), or "irrevocable," as most modern versions put it—meaning that spirituality has nothing to do with obtaining or keeping a gift—the opposite is true with entering into spiritual warfare as Paul outlines it in Ephesians 6:10–18.

Having stressed the importance of doing away with bitterness and totally forgiving those who have hurt us (Eph. 4:30–32), Paul stresses the importance and implications of sexual purity (Eph. 5:1–28). He then urges that husbands love their wives as their own bodies (Eph. 5:28) and bondservants respect their masters (Eph. 6:5–9). It is at this juncture that he says, "Finally, be strong in the Lord and in the strength of his might" (Eph. 6:10). Like it or not, he is not dealing with a spiritual gift in the rest of the Book of Ephesians but with a close relationship with the Lord Jesus. Knowing what he will say regarding spiritual warfare being defensive, he sets the stage for the evil day by telling us to be *strong in the Lord.*

It is a grim reminder that since the gifts are retained without repentance or obedience, they are therefore no indication of one's spirituality. King Saul was given the gift of prophecy (1 Sam. 10:9–12), which he never lost. On his way to kill young David we find that his gift was in good working order—prophesying (1 Sam. 19:24). In a day in which some (sadly) emphasize gifting over character— accompanied too often also with immorality and financial irresponsibility—the same people are often seen posing as experts in spiritual warfare. It is my opinion that God is fed up with this.

All that follows in Ephesians 6 is based upon the assumption that spiritual warfare is defensive. We saw earlier that the word *stand,* used four times, shows this. But not only that; all of the descriptions show that we are not the offense but the defense. We take our "stand" with the "whole armor of God." Furthermore:

- "Having fastened on the belt of truth" (v. 14). A belt holds all the armor together. Belt of *truth* means that to be able to withstand the devil in the evil day one must be sure that God defends "truth" vis-à-vis Satan, who is the father of lies (John 8:44). It shows too that we must know what we believe and why! We are confident when

we know that truth is on our side and that
we are on the side of truth.

- "Having put on the breastplate of righteousness" (v. 14). We are protected by the blood of Jesus and the imputed righteousness of God. That defense covering is what gives us confidence. If it were our own personal righteousness, which may vacillate from day to day, we would be ill-equipped to withstand Satan. But Christ's righteousness assures us that we are on solid ground. A hymn is relevant here:

My hope is built on nothing less than Jesus' blood
    and righteousness.
I dare not trust the sweetest frame but wholly
    lean on Jesus' name.
On Christ the solid rock I stand, all other ground
    is sinking sand.
               —EDWARD MOTE (1797–1874)[1]

- "As shoes for your feet, having put on the readiness given by the gospel of peace" (v. 15). We are not barefooted. We need to be ready to move. Prepared. The gospel of peace is understood in two ways: the peace with God (our justification) and the peace of God (the sense of His presence).

- "In all circumstances take up the shield of faith" (v. 16). A shield is for protection when we are being attacked. In the evil day we therefore have the shield as protection. A shield of "faith" is when we know how to "extinguish all the flaming darts of the evil one." Satan is our accuser; he will try to undermine our confidence in Jesus' blood. He will remind us of every fault we have. Here is another relevant hymn, this one by John Newton: "Be thou my shield and hiding place, that, sheltered near thy side, I may my fierce accuser face, and tell him thou hast died."[2]

- "Take the helmet of salvation" (v. 17). As the helmet fits on the head, so this refers to our mind. This means clear thinking. Sound doctrine. If anyone does do God's will they shall be able to know truth from error (John 7:17). However, because Paul refers to the helmet of "salvation" he wants to put his seal on what he has taught earlier in this book: that salvation is by grace through faith, not of ourselves; not of works lest we boast (Eph. 2:8–9).

- "The sword of the Spirit, which is the word of God" (v. 17). Out of Jesus' mouth came a "sharp two-edged sword" (Rev. 1:16). The New Testament loves the analogy of God's Word as a two-edged sword (Heb. 4:12). This also shows how *rhema* (Eph.

6:17) and *logos* (Heb. 4:12) can be used interchangeably.

- "Praying at all times in the Spirit" (v. 18). Jude refers to "praying in the Holy Spirit" (Jude 20). Paul says that when we do not know what to pray for, the Holy Spirit intercedes for us "with groanings too deep for words" (Rom. 8:26). Does this mean praying in tongues? Almost certainly. It corresponds to Paul's teaching in 1 Corinthians 14:2.

- "With all prayer and supplication" (v. 18). Paul refers to both prayer and supplication (e.g., petitioning) in Philippians 4:6. Keep in mind that these verses in Ephesians 6:14–18 are what prepare us for the evil day. In other words, don't wait until the evil day comes to start praying. It may be too late then! Maintain a solid, consistent prayer life alongside all else that Paul puts to us.

It is hard to know at what point Paul finishes his instructions for our preparation because he says, "And also for me" (v. 19). I take it that he has changed the subject.

## THE WAY FORWARD SUMMED UP

First, I suggest you pray daily for the sprinkling of the blood of Jesus. I speak for myself. After a cup of tea or coffee each morning I claim the promise that we should "believe the love" God has for us (1 John 4:16) and simultaneously ask for God's mercy (Heb. 4:16). I have done this for years. We never outgrow the need to ask for His mercy. Then I pray for the sprinkling of the blood of Jesus to rest on me. Why? For cleansing and for clear thinking.

The sprinkling of the blood of Christ is stated explicitly two times in the New Testament and one other time implicitly: (1) The writer of Hebrews says that in prayer we approach Jesus and "the sprinkled blood" (Heb. 12:24). This refers to the heavenly mercy where the blood of Christ was sprinkled (Heb. 9:5); (2) Peter refers to obedience to Jesus Christ and "for the sprinkling with his blood" (1 Pet. 1:2). What does this mean? By the Holy Spirit applying the blood we *continue* to enjoy the benefit of the blood of Christ. Jesus died once for all. This secures our eternal salvation. But because we have an ongoing relationship with God, the blood is applied for continued cleansing; (3) John teaches this implicitly in that if we walk in the light as God is in the light, we have fellowship with Him and "the blood of Jesus his Son cleanses us from all sin" (1 John 1:7).

When you know that the devil hates something, doing the opposite will be wise. Satan hates the blood of Jesus for reasons we have shown earlier—namely, it led to his downfall. Furthermore, we overcome by the blood of the Lamb and the word of our testimony.

Second, know who your real enemy is. When Paul

said that we wrestle not against flesh and blood, he was saying, "My enemy is not a human being." He could say, "My enemy is not Alexander the coppersmith or Demas." (See 2 Timothy 4:10, 14.) This is partly why he could say, "We wrestle not against flesh and blood"; some may do this, but not me! And yet the devil will try to get you to focus on people—on individuals who are trying to bring you down.

I have had a good number of trials and testings in my ministry of sixty-five years. In my early days, I am ashamed to admit, I focused on this person or that person. But I eventually came to see that this is precisely what the devil wanted me to do. He can influence our enemy to say hurtful and harmful things. I remember that in 1963 in my church in Carlisle, Ohio, there was a man in the church who hated my preaching on the deity of Jesus. He even said he preferred reading *The Watchtower* (the Jehovah's Witness magazine) to my weekly flyer called *Fairview Flame*. I then regarded him personally as my enemy. But Paul would slap my wrist today and say, "No. That man is not the enemy. The enemy is Satan!" I have learned a bit more about spiritual warfare since then.

Third, dignify every trial. This fulfills Paul's exhortation, "Be strong in the Lord." How does one become strong in the Lord? Learn the secret of thankfulness. God loves gratitude. He hates ingratitude. Gratitude must be taught. I have learned gratitude largely by learning to dignify trials. I blush to confess that I was a grumbler and murmurer of the worst kind for a long time.

Dignifying the trial means just what the phrase implies: you treat a trial with respect, honor, and dignity. After all, it is from God! A promise for joy! Hang on to these words from the extraordinary hymn "Like a River, Glorious":

> Every joy or trial, falleth from above,
> Traced upon our dial by the Sun of love.
> We may trust Him fully, all for us to do;
> They who trust Him wholly find Him wholly true.
> —FRANCES R. HAVERGAL (1836–1879)[3]

Here are six principles to follow:

1. Welcome it; accept it; don't reject it. From the beginning treat the trial as you would an angel knocking on your door.

2. Know that it is from God with a purpose; it is not for nothing. It will be clear one day.

3. Remember that every trial has a built-in time span; it will end. It could end suddenly. God knows the end from the beginning.

4. Thank God for trusting you with this precious opportunity. You are special. It may never come back like this again

5. Don't grumble. Don't utter a negative word throughout its time span. As the old spiritual put it: on the cross Jesus never uttered a "mumbling word."

6. Don't try to hasten its end; get the full benefit of God's plan for you in this testing. Don't live with the regret that you aborted the trial before it was over.

Fourth, I return to total forgiveness. We started with this; we end with it. If I have learned *anything* from being a pastor or preacher in my lifetime, it is that no one outgrows the need for repeated reminders along this line. I'm sorry, but it is needed everywhere. Why? Because we forget too soon!

The Lord's Prayer, in my candid opinion, should be prayed daily—not from rapid memory when it does not get uttered *from the heart,* but when we mean what we pray. When Jesus finished teaching the disciples this prayer in the Sermon on the Mount (Matt. 6:8–13), He added one application: "For if you forgive others their trespasses, your heavenly Father will also forgive you, but if you do not forgive others their trespasses, neither will your Father forgive your trespasses" (Matt. 6:14–15). This application, given immediately after this historic prayer, shows the most important thing about the prayer. It is almost as if this were the very reason for the prayer!

The petition for forgiveness in the Lord's Prayer is that we might have continued unbroken fellowship with the Father. It is not a prayer for salvation; neither is it a condition of salvation. It is the way forward to inherit the kingdom of heaven—the theme of the Sermon on the Mount. It is the way, the only way, to experience and enjoy the un-grieved Holy Spirit.

Forgiveness then must be continual; it is a life commitment. I call it a "life sentence," like when your physician prescribes a pill and says, "You will need to take this tablet the rest of your life." So too is forgiveness. It is the best antidote I know to thwart the plans of the devil. He has a plan. "Every time you forgive you disappoint the devil," said Rick Warren. Keep doing that!

# Conclusion

FEAR CAN BE good, bad, or ugly. When we fear man, we are more concerned with what others think than with what God thinks. This most often leads to depression and failure. Satanic fear is even worse; it produces demonic oppression and sometimes even death. But the fear of God leads us to peace. It creates a sense of awe that makes us aware of how real God is, and that awareness leads us to true knowledge and wisdom.

Fear doesn't have to rule your life. When you make the fear of God your greatest priority, you can walk free of ungodly fear. Step out in courage and truly trust God and His promises. Resolve to please the Lord and get your self-esteem from winning God's approval. When you do this, the fear of man loses its power over you and you are able to live boldly in Christ Jesus.

This is my prayer for you. May God the Father, God the Son, and God the Holy Spirit be with you and abide with you now and forever. Amen.

# Notes

INTRODUCTION

1. John Newton, "Amazing Grace! (How Sweet the Sound)," Hymnary.org, 1779, https://hymnary.org/text/amazing_grace_how_sweet_the_sound.

CHAPTER 1

1. Yogi Berra, BrainyQuote, accessed September 13, 2021, https://www.brainyquote.com/quotes/yogi_berra_100084.

2. Fanny Crosby, "Pass Me Not, O Gentle Savior," Hymnary.org, 1868, https://hymnary.org/text/pass_me_not_o_gentle_savior.

CHAPTER 3

1. William M. Greathouse, *The Fullness of the Spirit* (Kansas City, MO: Nazarene Publishing House, 1958).

CHAPTER 4

1. Dr. Josef Tson is an evangelist and the former president of the Romanian Missionary Society.

CHAPTER 5

1. Helen Howarth Lemmel, "Turn Your Eyes Upon Jesus," Hymnary.org, 1922, https://hymnary.org/text/o_soul_are_you_weary_and_troubled.

2. Charles Spurgeon (@Spurgeon_), "I looked at Christ, and the dove of peace filled my heart. I looked at the dove, and it flew away," reposted on Twitter, January 24, 2016, 9:48 p.m., https://twitter.com/spurgeon_/status/691452622876905473?lang=en.

3. W. Somerset Maugham, *Of Human Bondage* (New York: George H. Doran Co., 1915).

4. William Shakespeare, *Hamlet*, Act 1, Scene 3, 78–82, accessed September 22, 2021, https://www.enotes.com/shakespeare-quotes/thine-own-self-true.

## CHAPTER 6

1. John Piper, *Risk Is Right: Better to Lose Your Life Than to Waste It* (Wheaton, IL: Crossway, 2013).

2. "Article #5," Christian History Institute, accessed September 23, 2021, https://christianhistoryinstitute.org/incontext/article/ignatius.

3. "Article #7," Christian History Institute, accessed September 23, 2021, https://christianhistoryinstitute.org/incontext/article/polycarp-testimony.

4. "Hugh Latimer," Wikiquote, accessed September 23, 2021, https://en.wikiquote.org/wiki/Hugh_Latimer.

5. "John Bradford: English Reformer and Martyr," Christian Classics Ethereal Library, accessed

September 23, 2021, https://www.ccel.org/ccel/
bradford.

## CHAPTER 7

1. Charles Creitz, "Cardinal Dolan Shares Pope
   Francis' Message for Coronavirus-Ravaged NYC,"
   Fox News, April 16, 2020, https://www.foxnews.
   com/media/cardinal-dolan-pope-francis-message-
   nyc-coronavirus.

## CHAPTER 8

1. "Martyn Lloyd-Jones Quotes," AZ Quotes,
   accessed October 6, 2021, https://www.azquotes
   .com/quote/1403740.

## CHAPTER 10

1. Edward Mote, "My Hope Is Built on Nothing
   Less," Hymnary.org, 1834, https://hymnary.org/
   text/my_hope_is_built_on_nothing_less.

2. John Newton, "Pleading His Gracious Name,"
   Hymnary.org, 1779, https://hymnary.org/text/
   approach_my_soul_the_mercy_seat.

3. Frances R. Havergal, "Like a River, Glorious,"
   Timeless Truths, 1876, https://library.timelesstruths
   .org/music/Like_a_River_Glorious/.